The Dragon's Tail

A VOLUME IN THE SERIES

Culture, Politics, and the Cold War

EDITED BY

Christian G. Appy

The Dragon's Tail
Americans Face the Atomic Age

Robert A. Jacobs

University of Massachusetts Press

AMHERST AND BOSTON

Copyright © 2010 by University of Massachusetts Press
All rights reserved
Printed in the United States of America

LC 2009048475
ISBN 978-1-55849-727-6 (paper); 726-9 (library cloth)

Designed by Dean Bornstein
Set in Warnock Pro
Printed and bound by Thomson-Shore, Inc.

Library of Congress Cataloging-in-Publication Data

Jacobs, Robert A., 1960–
    The dragon's tail : Americans face the atomic age / Robert A. Jacobs.
        p. cm. — (Culture, politics, and the Cold War)
    Includes bibliographical references and index.
    ISBN 978-1-55849-727-6 (paper : alk. paper) — ISBN 978-1-55849-726-9 (library
cloth : alk. paper)
    1. United States—Civilization—1945– 2. United States—Civilization—1945—
Sources. 3. Atomic bomb—Social aspects—United States—History—20th century.
4. Atomic bomb—Social aspects—United States—History—20th century—
Sources. 5. Nuclear warfare—Social aspects—United States—History—20th
century. 6. Nuclear warfare—Social aspects—United States—History—20th
century—Sources. 7. War and society—United States—History—20th century.
8. War and society—United States—History—20th century—Sources. 9. Social
change—United States—History—20th century. 10. Social change—United
States—History—20th century—Sources. I. Title.
    E169.12.J265 2010
    973.91—dc22

                                                        2009048475

British Library Cataloguing in Publication data are available.

For my mother, Muriel Jacobs,
and my children, Kaya, Ocea,
Gwynneth, and Levi Jacobs.

Contents

Illustrations

Acknowledgments

In Doris Lessing's second Canopus book, *The Marriages Between Zones Three, Four and Five*, the children born in Zone Three were all considered to have many, even a dozen, parents. This book, like a child in Zone Three, has countless parents and even a few siblings. The greatest debt of gratitude is to Lillian Hoddeson, without whose guidance and criticism this book would never have been born. Her wisdom, practicality, and kindness are present on every page. Earlier versions of this book benefited from the advice of many people. Most important among them are Mark Leff and Leslie Reagan at the University of Illinois and David Noble and Roger Jones at the University of Minnesota. Ruth Hein provided clear and coherent editing, and Mark Selden offered critical advice and guidance in bringing the book to press, as did my colleagues at the Hiroshima Peace Institute (HPI) Narayanan Ganesan, Sung Chull Kim, and Hiroko Takahashi. Mick Broderick also provided critical feedback on several chapters and invaluable moral support. The administrative staff at HPI has given endless support to my work on this book, and I especially want to thank HPI President Motofumi Asai for his continual support and enthusiasm.

I also must say, as a scholar publishing my first single-author book, that the horror stories of academic publishing made me nervous. But my experience with the staff at the University of Massachusetts Press has been fantastic from the very start. The support and professional guidance of Clark Dougan, senior editor, and Bruce Wilcox, director, could not have been better as they steered this neophyte through the publishing process. And the sharp editorial eye and knife of Mary Bellino brought crispness to the prose that turned each revision into an English class for me.

The debt to my family and friends for their support, love, and advice during the writing of this book can never be adequately stated. My children, Kaya, Ocea, Gwynne, and Levi have all referred to this book as the fifth child for most of their lives and are happy to see their sibling finally be born. Their love and dedication to my work has given me strength every single day, and their support radiates from every word printed here. Likewise my mother, Muriel Jacobs, and my wife, Carol Agrimson, have kept me whole and moving forward through so many challenges. My best friends, Brian Johnson and Julie Gordon, have loved and supported me through the writing of this book in so many ways that I lost count. Thanks also to many others who have helped make this book possible, specifically my brother Jay Jacobs, Mike and Joe Jacobs, Danny Clark, Jeb Binsted, Jeff St. Andrews, Lon Haber, Yolanda Sala, Billie Jo Vinson, Audrey and Jimmy and Emma and Abby Wyatt, Kara and Siera and Elle Stevens, Tracy Jacobs, Al Rose, Rhonda Welbel, and of course David Razowsky. And finally, my thanks to the late Hamza El Din, whose music provided the background to the writing of this book and who was one of the first people to call me "doctor" after my doctorate was awarded; that was a true honor.

My debt to you all can never be repaid, and my joy in experiencing such community and such love can never be quantified. It has created me, sustained me, and brought me to this day.

The Dragon's Tail

Introduction

At the Core of the Bomb, Narratives

> It is an atomic bomb. It is a harnessing
> of the basic power of the universe.
>
> *President Harry S. Truman, August 6, 1945*

Of the thousands of experiments conducted at the Los Alamos lab during the Manhattan Project, one has become emblematic of our encounter with nuclear weapons. It was called "tickling the dragon's tail," and it was critical to the successful construction of the first atomic bombs, the one tested at Trinity in New Mexico in July 1945 and the two dropped on Hiroshima and Nagasaki the following month. The experiment claimed lives in Los Alamos and enabled the taking of hundreds of thousands more in Japan.

Tickling the dragon's tail was a means of determining what quantity of plutonium or uranium-235 was required to make a nuclear reaction go critical (that is, for a nuclear chain reaction to start) and therefore to cause a nuclear explosion. Too little, and the bomb wouldn't work; too much, and precious wartime resources might be wasted. The experiment was designed to provide information about this threshold by bringing subcritical amounts of bomb material together until it was clear what quantity was sufficient.

In the poetic naming of this experiment by physicist Richard Feynman, who originally called it "tickling the tail of a sleeping dragon," the humans were doing the tickling, and the dormant power inside the atom was the sleeping dragon.[1] But as the image implies, there was always a danger that the awakened dragon might be a force too powerful to be controlled. When this indeed came to pass, less poetic people would call this state of affairs *the atomic age.*

Taking this step, seeking to acquire this power, was almost irresistible: J. Robert Oppenheimer admitted that one reason scientists engaged in this work was that it was "technically sweet."[2] Even after Manhattan Project scientists obtained the information they needed to successfully manufacture and detonate the two nuclear weapons used on Japanese cities in 1945, they were not yet done with the dragon. The experiment continued, and in the year after World War II ended, two project scientists would die from accidents that occurred while tickling the dragon's tail.

While initially the experiment was conducted by scientists, now it is conducted by governments, by nonstate actors, and by rogues—scientists as well as regimes. We are all collectively gathered in the laboratory, holding our breaths, hoping, dreading: we fear that our encounter with the dragon might also become a criticality accident, just as it did for the two Los Alamos scientists. The sleeping dragon has awakened and turned to face us, and now we circle each other slowly through the decades, through the incidents. We sometimes tell ourselves that the dragon will destroy us, but at other times we tell ourselves that the dragon may yet set us free. It is a story whose ending we write with our lives, with our choices.

This book is about stories, nuclear stories. Stories of how Americans came to understand nuclear weapons and what they imagined a nuclear war would be like. Stories that the U.S. government told to its own citizens and soldiers, and stories told in movie theaters and on the radio.

The poet and historian John Canaday reminds us that the bomb began as a story. Referring to H. G. Wells's 1914 novel *The World Set Free*, which predicted an atomic war in the year 1956, Canaday writes that "before they became physical facts, atomic weapons existed as literary fictions."[3] "The nuclear powers have built atomic weapons not because they want to employ them in combat," Canaday notes, "but they have continued to develop, construct, maintain, and deploy these bombs for symbolic ends. By representing the massive death and destruction they might cause, they are meant to render their physical use superfluous. In effect, atomic weapons are useful because of the stories people tell about them, the fears those stories inspire, and the actions by which people respond to those fears."[4]

The Cold War was a period of history profoundly shaped by a physical object—the bomb—that very few people had actually ever seen. What gave them nightmares of nuclear explosions, what compelled them to dig underground fallout shelters, and what led them to fund the nuclear arms race were *stories* about the bomb. These stories were told in articles by "experts" who predicted that the advent of nuclear weapons would lead either to the end of the world or to a world of peace and plenty; in apocalyptic denunciations of the evil designs of the hated Soviet enemy by government and military officials; in science fiction tales of the last survivor of an imagined nuclear war; even in a cartoon tale of a turtle who taught children how to survive an atomic attack.

Nuclear weapons are very real. They have killed hundreds of thousands, if not millions, of people, and exposure to radiation from nuclear weapons continues to claim victims every year. By the U.S. government's own reckoning, fallout from atmospheric nuclear weapons testing in the late 1950s resulted in the presence of measurable radiation in the teeth and bones of all humans on the earth and in much of the milk supply.[5] The very real threat of a "push-button war" that would destroy the cities of both warring nations and produce sufficient radiological toxicity to threaten all human life also exacted a heavy toll on the mental health of humankind. But even these realities are presented in narrative form— they are stories about the present dangers. This is the form in which most Americans encountered the nuclear threat (not forgetting, of course, that they were also encountering it as fallout and as tax burden).

Since the introduction of the bomb to the American public in 1945, there has been a primary nuclear narrative in which the bomb functions as a signifier of social transformation. This narrative emerged from the rhetoric that explained the bomb in 1945 and 1946. I call this primary narrative of nuclear culture the *alchemical narrative*—alchemical because of the strong emphasis on nuclear weapons as signifiers of transformation or fundamental change. This alchemical narrative told a fundamental story about the atomic age: it was a turning point for human society; it was an age of transformation. To people around the world, nuclear weapons announced that the past was gone and the future had arrived.[6]

From the very start of the atomic age, nuclear narratives spilled over into the fantastic: atomic power might lead to an age of limitless energy and abundance, making physical labor unnecessary; it might make war obsolete; it might fill the natural world with unnatural genetic mutants; it might lead to horrifying destruction and the end of the world, and the flash of a bomb might be the last thing you and most other people on the earth would ever see. Whether the expectation was dystopian or utopian, the bomb affected a rupture, separating the normality of the past from the uncertainty of the future—a marker that we had entered a transformed—and transformative—landscape.

Stories are central to an understanding of the impact the advent of nuclear weapons has had on society. When President Harry Truman introduced the bomb to the American public, he told a story about atomic

energy—that it was the "basic power of the universe," the source of the
sun's energy, and that this fundamental key to the limitless power hidden
in the natural world was specifically given to his country "by God."[7] The
rapid end of World War II further substantiated the pedigree of the bomb
as a mysterious agent of divine will, dispatched from heaven to alter the
course of human events—in fact, to intervene on the side of the
Americans.

Within days of the news from Hiroshima, even before World War II
had formally ended, social commentators spoke of entering the "Atomic
Age" and speculated with dread and wonder about the future. Political
cartoonists filled the newspapers with depictions of the bomb confronting the world with unimagined new dangers. By the end of August 1945,
Pocket Books had already published a paperback titled *The Atomic Age
Opens.*[8]

Writing just hours after the announcement of the detonation of the
Hiroshima bomb, Norman Cousins, the thirty-three-year-old editor of
the *Saturday Review of Literature*, declared that "modern man is obsolete." Cousins worried that "man stumbles fitfully into a new era of atomic energy for which he is as ill equipped to accept its potential blessings
as he is to control its present dangers." He warned that society was at a
crossroads where a choice would be made between global destruction
and social transformation, and he saw the battle for the life or death of
society in the atomic age being fought on the battleground of the human
self. Modern man had evolved to the point where he could build an atomic bomb, but unless human collective social conscience evolved as fully
as our technological abilities, society was doomed. The scope of this
challenge cast a "blanket of obsolescence not only over the methods and
products of man but over man himself."[9]

Like Cousins, the American public tried to understand what it meant
to have entered the atomic age. The actual mechanics of the physics
involved were difficult for nonscientists to grasp. Some of the ideas, such
as the presence of enormous energies in atomic nuclei, or the curvature
of time-space, seemed irrational from an everyday, experiential perspective. Nature suddenly appeared to be a very abstract place, one in which
the common-sense laws of Newtonian physics had given way to a threatening world beyond perception. One of the ways Americans learned to
understand such atomic icons as *radiation* was as signifiers of a new
vision of the physical world, a vision in which forces operated beyond
perception, where time and space were not fixed.

Cousins codified the essence of the first nuclear narrative: the bomb would either destroy the world or transform it. Human technological abilities seemed to have far outpaced human social abilities, and if society did not change quickly, atomic weapons would certainly bring a war to end civilization. Human society was at a fork in the road: one path led to atomic holocaust, the other to a future of peace and plenty. This was the nuclear dilemma: navigating past the danger and accomplishing the transformation.

Just a few days after the bombing of Hiroshima, an editorial in the *New York Times* revealed the depth and power of the alchemical narrative at the dawning moments of the atomic age. It stated clearly that even with World War II coming to a close, the biggest challenge to human society lay ahead: "Even the inevitable end of a great war cannot wholly lift from men's hearts the burden that was laid upon them last Sunday by the dropping of an atomic bomb on the Japanese city of Hiroshima. By their own cruelty and treachery our enemies have invited the worst we can do to them. Even so, no one can fail to realize that by this invention and this act humanity has been brought face to face with the most awful crisis in its recorded history. *Here the long pilgrimage of man on earth turns towards darkness or towards light.*"[10]

In 1937 the physicist and nuclear pioneer Ernest Rutherford published the first book on atomic physics that used the title *The New Alchemy*. Frederick Soddy, who along with Rutherford first correctly determined the mechanism of natural radioactivity, exclaimed at the time of that discovery, "Rutherford! This is transmutation!" Soddy was characterizing the phenomenon of radiation as the result of the transmutation of atoms from one element into another, thus achieving the long-fabled changing of one form of matter into another that was at the core of the medieval alchemical enterprise. In his research into the cross-cultural contamination of nuclear physics and the concurrent revival of occultism in Europe, the historian Mark Morrison has found that "by the 1920s, atomic physics and radiochemistry were regularly called 'modern alchemy' in the press."[11]

This identification of nuclear science with alchemy and with the magical worldview (suggested by the new scientific narrative of a world beyond sensory experience) endows nuclear iconography with a profound sense of the supernatural. To this day, this aura of magic still surrounds nuclear icons as they appear in popular culture. Nuclear imagery became an alembic, and whatever specific nuclear icon emerged into popular culture would function in part as a signifier of the new magic and of the potential for transformation.

The iconography of radiation provides an apt demonstration of the point. The human body cannot sense radiation; we can receive a lethal dose without being in the least aware of danger. Unlike the instant impact of blast or fire, radiation can work slowly, but it is no less deadly. Radiation also produces genetic mutations. Precisely because it is an imperceptible force that can kill or transform without any sign of damage, radiation has been the most terrifying of all the effects of nuclear weapons and the one that U.S. policymakers long suppressed in all public discussions of the bomb. In science fiction films of the 1950s, this reality led naturally to the use of radiation as an all-powerful marker of transformation. If a movie opened with a shot of someone holding a Geiger counter that emitted an ominous "click, click, click," then no matter what came next—giant bugs, half human–half lobsters, aliens, people walking through walls—there was no need to explain how such an anomaly could have come about: radiation made anything believable; it was a cultural marker to indicate that a supernatural threshold had been crossed. These stories were frequently counternarratives about the dangers of radiation. While many Americans may not have understood geneticists' warnings about the dangers of mutation from radioactive fallout, they responded viscerally to movie images of fifty-foot-tall spiders bent on destruction.

While many scholars have pointed out that the alchemical thread was only one of several important nuclear narrative threads, I would argue that it was the one that dominated cultural expressions of nuclear iconography. Subsequent nuclear narratives often contained the basic transformative message of the alchemical narrative, which functioned as a master narrative. This alchemical narrative was woven into cultural expressions of other nuclear narratives, such as ways to survive a nuclear explosion, the nature of fallout, or the role of radiation in genetic mutations. Stories that included nuclear themes were stories about change, about alternative possibilities. Nuclear iconology denoted a transformed state—nuclear wars reset calendars to "year zero," points of impact for nuclear explosions were "ground zero," midnight on the nuclear "doomsday clock" marked the end of time, and movie screens showed mutant survivors no longer bound by the rules of humanity and mutated bugs and reptiles that inverted the natural order of the food chain. The irradiated landscape was one in which the world was turned on its head, one where established rules could be rewritten.

This is what many scholars of nuclear culture and history miss: the *primacy* of this mythic experience of nuclear weapons for most Americans. While they do note the "transformative" nature of nuclear stories, it is generally depicted as one of many strands of nuclear culture, like the possibility of nuclear trains or cars, or the promise of nuclear power. Narratives about better appliances and lower electricity bills in the future are simply not equivalent to narratives about the annihilation of any future at all. Spencer Weart has pointed out the ubiquitous presence of older mythical tropes in nuclear iconography.[12] This is precisely because the visceral experience of the advent of these weapons for most Americans was a breakdown of the normalcy of their life's story, and an entrance into mythic space.

⫸⫷

One question that has been central to scholarship about nuclear culture is how "new" nuclear icons really are. How new were fears of a threat that could end the world? And how new were the stories that expressed that fear?

The discussion of the *newness* of nuclear culture is provoked by the clearly revolutionary nature of the weapons themselves. There was no doubt about the shocking nature of these weapons when they emerged into public awareness in 1945. Very few people had even heard of nuclear physics, let alone possessed a working knowledge of its potential. The destruction in Hiroshima and Nagasaki was achieved by utilizing the energy inside the nucleus of the atom, a source of power almost completely unknown and even unimagined outside of a small group of scientists.

Most Americans were shocked when they heard the news of the bombing of Hiroshima on August 6, 1945. The subsequent rapid surrender by the Japanese imperial government in a war that many Americans had expected to continue for at least another brutal, bloody year reinforced the perception of a radical new weapon of unimaginable power. This fact has naturally led some scholars to assert that nuclear culture was a new phenomenon, essentially because it responded to a new phenomenon. Paul Boyer has written that in his study of the nuclear culture in the years immediately after the bombings of Hiroshima and Nagasaki, he was surprised by "how quickly contemporary observers understood that a profoundly unsettling new cultural factor had been introduced—that the bomb had transformed not only military strategy and international relations, but the fundamental ground of culture and consciousness."[13] Spencer Weart argues that while the weapon was shockingly new, mental frameworks with which to understand it followed well-worn paradigms: "Modern thinking about nuclear energy employs imagery that can be traced back to a time long before the discovery of radioactivity."[14] Weart meticulously examines the presence of archetypal antecedents encoded in the imagery of modern nuclear culture.

The sensibility that Weart posits is not itself new. Cousins wrote after hearing Truman's Hiroshima declaration: "The beginning of the Atomic Age has brought less hope than fear. It is a primitive fear, the fear of the unknown—the fear of forces man can neither channel nor comprehend. This fear is not new; in its classical form it is the fear of irrational death. It has burst out of the subconscious and into the conscious, filling the mind with primordial apprehensions."[15] But even as Cousins argued that the fear that gripped humans on that Monday night was not new, he claimed that the new weapon had made modern man *obsolete.*

Apocalyptic culture is as old as religious belief, and its antecedents can be traced throughout the imagery of nuclear culture, but some striking and profound new elements illustrated the threat posed by and the reaction to nuclear weapons. First and foremost, traditional narratives of an end-time were predicated on divine or supernatural intervention in the human world. The world came to an end by the action of a god or demon, perhaps in response to human actions or inadequacies, but humans at best provoked the divine: they were not powerful enough themselves to accomplish the apocalypse. In the atomic age, belief in the possible end of the world was based on an existing technology currently in the hands of human beings. In fact, it was imagined that the individual leaders of nuclear-armed nations themselves had a finger on the button that could end the world. What was new, then, was not the notion of the end of the world but the awareness that this outcome had become a real power in the hands—the fingertips—of actual humans. No longer was the struggle for the life and death of human civilization cast as a matter of convincing the gods that humans were worthy, or faithful, or moral. Now the continued existence of the world seemed to depend on the whims of our all-too-human leaders. This was a different matter entirely.

Although Harry Truman thanked God on August 6, 1945, for delivering the atomic bomb into our hands rather than those of our enemies, God saw fit to deliver it into their hands a mere four years later.[16] Even if Americans could convince themselves of the virtues of their leaders, what could it portend for the world to have the power to end life on earth in the hands of a brutal dictator like Stalin? People who had seen two world wars in their own lifetimes had little reason to be optimistic that such apocalyptic powers in the hands of political and military leaders would be handled with the omniscience one might expect of a god. Even for triumphalist Americans, who felt that their military had fought on the side of morality in World War II, not far behind that vision was the memory of such actions as the Bonus March of 1932, when the U.S. Army fired on veterans of World War I who were seeking early payment of their bonuses in the midst of the Great Depression. Human beings, with all their obvious frailties and irrationalities, now possessed destructive physical powers previously reserved for gods, and this was reason to be worried. It was indeed a new world.

Another element that changed radically was our conception of the future. Fundamental to human culture was the concept of the continuity of past, present, and future. Conceptual breaks in this continuity, in the form of apocalyptic or millennial narratives, indicated that any disruption between the present and the future was affected by human behavior (through the virtue or sinfulness of society) but was in the control of divine beings. It was all part of a divine plan. Humans were actors in this plan, but a god or gods were in control of the options. The nuclear future seemed totally uncontrollable; there might be giant mutated bugs and animals hunting humans, there might be gigantic or deformed people, there might be a world devoid of human life altogether, there might even be a *Jetsons*-like world of abundance and technology. But there no longer appeared to be any narrative continuity in popular depictions of the future, only improvisation.

The specific history of nuclear testing is the key to understanding the distinctions between different periods of nuclear culture in the United States during the early Cold War. Within this history, further distinctions may be made, but the essential break separating the earlier from the later period of nuclear culture is the shifting of nuclear testing from atmospheric tests to underground testing as a result of the Partial Test Ban Treaty of 1963.[17]

The atmospheric testing of nuclear weapons made them a very real part of Americans' daily world. First there is the visual element: testing bombs in the atmosphere results in visible mushroom clouds, and the iconic image of the mushroom cloud was synonymous with the notion of the bomb itself. Peter B. Hales, a historian of architecture and art, writes that "the central icon of the atomic culture is the mushroom cloud . . . ; it has become so deeply imprinted in the myths and matrices of the postwar era that it has come to seem natural, a fundamental, even a necessary aspect of everyday life."[18]

During the atmospheric testing era, newspapers and magazines accompanied reports of nuclear weapons tests in Nevada and in the Pacific with images of the resulting mushroom clouds. "The image of an atomic explosion, usually represented by a photograph of a mushroom cloud," the art critic Vincent Leo notes, "has become an overwhelming visual presence in world culture."[19] Starting in 1952, many Nevada tests were televised and viewed in American homes. The ubiquitous presence of mushroom clouds in the news during the early Cold War years was a continual reminder of the presence and threat of nuclear weapons. The underground testing of nuclear weapons removed this most crucial visual reminder of the imminence of nuclear war. Reading a newspaper account of underground testing had little of the impact of a photograph of "the cloud at the end of the world."[20]

The second reason atmospheric testing confronted people with the reality of nuclear war in a way that differed from underground testing involves the health threat of radioactive fallout, which was very much less pronounced in relation to underground detonations. While many people had fears about nuclear war, radioactive fallout was already having a direct effect on the health of the people of the world as a result of atmospheric testing.

Public awareness of the dangers of fallout spread across the nation with the radiation from the Bravo test in March 1954. Bravo tested the first deliverable thermonuclear weapon (H-bomb) at the Pacific Proving Ground, and the resulting radiation contaminated a Japanese tuna trawler and several hundred Pacific islanders located more than a hundred miles from the blast's epicenter.[21] The resulting illnesses of those exposed became front-page news in the United States and led to the first public calls to end nuclear weapon testing. It was the Bravo test that put the word *fallout* into the public vocabulary.

In almost all the science fiction B-movies of the 1950s, it is weapons testing and not nuclear war that is the source of the supernatural threat. This is true of such primordial monster movies as *Godzilla* and *The Beast from 20,000 Fathoms*, and *Killers from Space* and other alien-invasion movies, and the giant bug movies such as *Them!*[22] This plethora of cinematic otherworldly menaces spawned by nuclear testing demonstrates the extent to which public anxiety about radioactive fallout, and about the presence of the bomb itself, was embodied by the atmospheric testing program. Again, when testing went underground, the monsters and aliens of the B-movies largely disappeared.

In the late 1950s and early 1960s, the National Committee for a Sane

Nuclear Policy (SANE), made public anxiety about the health threats posed by the atmospheric testing of nuclear weapons the focus of a very successful ad campaign aimed at generating public support for ending these tests.[23] The ads connected the dangers of radioactive fallout from weapons tests to the comforts of daily middle-class life. One pictured a milk bottle with a skull and crossbones denoting poison, another featured a pregnant woman with the claim that "1¼ Million unborn children will be born dead or have some gross defect because of Nuclear Bomb testing," while still another showed a group of happy, smiling children above the statement that "*Your* children's teeth contain Strontium-90."[24]

American's concerns over the health effects of radioactive fallout generated worries in the U.S. defense establishment that there would shortly be public calls for the closure of the Nevada Test Site. This thinking led to the U.S. government's willingness to sign the Partial Test Ban Treaty and thus shift nuclear weapon detonations to underground shafts. With nuclear weapons testing no longer visible in the same sky under which people lived their daily lives. increasingly dangerous weapons began to fade more and more from public view and consciousness.

During the era of aboveground testing, humans and the bomb shared the same atmosphere. Nuclear culture from this period is more intimate than the nuclear culture of the later underground-testing years. Even when antinuclear sentiment would strongly reassert itself during the nuclear freeze movement of the early 1980s, it would have a more generalized tone. It would not be a culture of hand-to-hand combat with giant bugs, of soldiers advancing from trenches toward mushroom clouds, or pilots named Kong riding H-bombs like bucking broncos. It would be a more depersonalized though more accurate culture of nuclear winter, of a mammal-free "republic of insects and grass" in which human agency had been carbonized, leaving no shadow.[25]

1

Atomic Familiars on the Radioactive Landscape

> "Oh my," thought the little piglet, "what will become of us all?"
>
> *Patty, the Atomic Pig (1951)*

Nuclear Radiation as a Cultural Icon

On what appears to be a normal day off the Pacific coast of California, Scott Thomas is relaxing on his boat and enjoying a peaceful day of leisure. His wife has just gone below to grab two beers when he notices a strange fog approaching. He stands up, and for a moment the fog envelops him. The cloud passes, and when his wife returns, she sees that Scott seems to be covered with glitter. The couple thinks nothing of the phenomenon until the impossible begins to happen: Thomas begins to shrink; he has been transformed into *The Incredible Shrinking Man.*[1]

Released in 1957 as public concern over radioactive fallout from nuclear weapons tests was rising, *The Incredible Shrinking Man* uses the device of a radioactive cloud from such a test as a plot twist. It causes Scott Thomas to become so tiny that he has to fight with cats and spiders. He shrinks out of his job, out of his marriage, out of his life. His exposure to radiation has a devolutionary impact on him: he fights a progressively smaller and smaller set of adversaries, until finally he becomes microbial. At no point do we see any form of destruction or horror; the only monster is the silent cloud of fallout. After Scott innocently notices it in the opening scene of the movie, it slowly and inexorably dehumanizes and erases him (fig. 1).

The monster postulated in this movie was a real monster; its clouds blew across the United States even as the movie was in theaters. Moviegoers could consider the notion that the fog in the air when they left the showing of *The Incredible Shrinking Man* might just be that real, live monster.

Radiation embodies some of the most paradoxical iconography of the early Cold War.[2] Its abstract nature (invisible, odorless, tasteless), when combined with its true dangers (genetic mutation, cancer, death), allows it to evoke impossible worlds emerging from the ordinary one. Able to kill silently and invisibly at a distance and, by the late 1950s, widely reputed to be present in mother's milk and human bones, radiation represented a

1. Scott Thomas faces the fallout cloud that will change his life in Universal Pictures' 1957 film *The Incredible Shrinking Man*.

threatening technological world that seemed to exist beyond reach of the senses.[3]

In the 1954 science fiction movie *Them!* radioactivity from the Trinity test turns ordinary ants into giant insects that roam the deserts of the Southwest, eventually filling the Los Angeles sewer system.[4] Radiation was a tool-in-trade for television, radio, movies, novels, and short stories as the strange force that authenticated any departure from normal space and time. It was the magic bullet of science fiction plots: passing a clicking Geiger counter across a scene was as good as waving a magic wand— be it giant bugs or bug-eyed aliens living in a vast underground city, the clicking made any plot twist believable. Radiation came to symbolize a break in the normal structure of everyday reality; it was a narrative marker to indicate that a boundary had been crossed and that from this moment on anything was possible.

Radiation was often used in popular culture to signify that the future had arrived. But the envisioned future was, as likely as not, a dystopia where insects are our ultimate competitors and the scale of our own human violence is measured in biblical terms. In the plot structure of science fiction movies, radiation is inevitably detected the instant before matters go awry. Not unlike the theatrical maxim that a gun seen on stage must go off by the third act, the clicking of a Geiger counter in a 1950s science fiction film was a sign that something technological was about to go terribly wrong and that objects and events that might otherwise seem physically impossible (such as invisible creatures that suck the brains out of unsuspecting humans) are almost certain to happen.

Radiation was the device employed in science fiction plots to make the emergence of monsters, both prehistoric ones and the products of genetic mutation, believable, and weapons testing was cited as the specific cause more frequently than nuclear war.[5] The Nevada desert, the continental site of U.S. nuclear weapons testing, became a symbolic landscape that granted alien beings and forces access to our world. The evil contained in the human psyche could also draw on radiation to gain unnatural power, threaten masses of humanity, and undermine social stability.[6] By the late 1950s, nuclear radiation had acquired a cultural iconography that was commonly used to legitimize departures from the bounds of reality in popular culture texts.

Central to the history of nuclear popular culture is the history of nuclear weapon testing. "The accidental awakening of the super-destructive monster, who has slept in the earth since prehistory, is, often, an obvious metaphor for the Bomb," Susan Sontag wrote in the early 1960s, but she also cited the additional importance of radiation and weapons testing: "Radiation casualties—ultimately, the conception of the whole world as a casualty of nuclear testing and nuclear warfare—is the most ominous of all the notions with which science fiction films deal."[7]

From the Bikini tests in 1946 through the entire atmospheric testing era (ending in 1963), nuclear weapons testing had a profound and multifaceted effect on American society and culture. In 1951, the Nevada Test Site (NTS) was established about seventy-five miles northwest of Las Vegas, and by the following year, Americans could watch tests on television right in their own homes. These broadcasts helped to establish a visual geography of the test site, which eventually became the backdrop for countless science fiction films.

During this period, the United States tested hundreds of nuclear weapons in the atmosphere, both in Nevada and in the Pacific Ocean at the Pacific Proving Ground (PPG). As a rule, less powerful (smaller, fission) weapons were tested in Nevada, while the stronger (larger, fusion) bombs were detonated at the PPG. The Pacific weapons had the most immediate and vivid effects on the health of human populations downwind from the explosions. In particular, it was the 1954 Bravo shot, with its immense fallout impact, that revealed that the world was quickly becoming highly radioactive and that people did not need to be aware of a nuclear explosion to end up as fallout casualties.

In the introduction, I also discussed the development of nuclear icons into signifiers of impending social transformation; the changed universe was presented either as the end of the world or as a futuristic Edenic age without need or war. It was only natural that such potent symbols, capable of rewriting the laws of physics as well as reconfiguring human society, would be employed in a broad range of cultural texts to signify both the power to transform and simply power itself. This trend can be seen in the many products that were assigned the name "atomic" in the late 1940s and early 1950s—for example, *Atomic* brand razor blades (ca. 1946–1950) and *Up n'Atom* brand carrots from M. L. Kalich and Company in Watsonville, California (ca. 1946–1950). It was also the perfect iconography for filmmakers and novelists in their attempts to lend credibility to explorations of impossible worlds. They had no need to laboriously invent the specifics of some science fiction setting; the simple invocation of radiation provided their constructs with legitimacy.

Nevada: "Where the Giant Mushrooms Grow"

Ten years and one day before opening day at Disneyland, the first nuclear weapon, Trinity, was tested in the New Mexico desert.[8] A trip to Disneyland offered access to Fantasyland and Tomorrowland, but for many Americans the real world in which they lived had become even more fantastic and futuristic.[9] The advent of nuclear weapons had altered the landscape in many ways: it challenged traditional narratives of the human future, even raising doubts as to whether there would be a future; it raised the possibility of radioactive poisoning or contamination on a global scale; it suggested that genetics could be toyed with, altering the balance of nature; and it put this power in the hands of human beings rather than in the hands of God.

As the invited guests crowded into Disneyland on that hot July day, the uninvited guest of radioactive fallout was visiting American homes in the area downwind of the fourteen nuclear weapons tests recently completed in Nevada.[10] The series of atomic tests at the NTS in 1955 was called Operation Teapot, a fitting name for the Alice-in-Wonderland world unfolding there, and in American popular culture as well. A few weekends spent in the local movie houses during those years would quickly reveal that the desert West was a mix of the Wild West, outer space, and some kind of primordial zoo populated with giant bugs, overgrown and violent reptiles, fifty-foot-tall men and women, and aliens with very cheap wardrobes.

This strange new world, in which the bizarre dangers of the atomic age seemed to draw humankind through Fantasyland and Tomorrowland and to the brink of oblivion, was not something dreamed up by B-movie producers and science fiction novelists. Rather, the setting and population of this world were cast from actual events and narratives conceived during the early years of the atomic age: it was the reality of nuclear weapons that drove the culture. By negating what had been held to be the basic laws of physics, nuclear icons implicitly suggested that other laws might turn out not to be absolute either. In this way, nuclear iconography became a set of gateway symbols: signifiers of the world that might exist beyond previously established boundaries. In popular culture, crossing this boundary into the fantastic brought one to Nevada.

During the atmospheric testing era, from 1945 to 1963, the United States detonated 317 nuclear weapons in the atmosphere, including 207 in Nevada, with a peak of more than 80 (between Nevada and the Pacific testing site) in 1962.[11] As the frequency of nuclear weapon testing increased, so too did public awareness of radiation and fallout. Test-ban advertisements, along with scattered news reports, reminded Americans that the world they lived in was increasingly radioactive.[12] Nevada, as the continental home of nuclear explosions, became a symbolic landscape in which radiation opened the United States to otherworldly forces. The frequent press reports and televising of nuclear tests in Nevada in the early 1950s helped to establish a visual iconography that would be used in the latter years of that decade by science fiction movies and other popular culture texts to evoke the transformed world of the nuclear future, forming what John G. Cawelti has called a symbolic landscape.[13]

The February 19, 1951, issue of *Newsweek* carried an unusual image "taken by the light of an atomic flash (fig. 2).[14] The light that illuminated the photograph, taken on the morning of February 6, came from an atomic explosion seventy-five miles away at the Nevada Test Site, but it shone as though from the future. The picture, which contains a Joshua tree and a wagon wheel as well as the atomic tourists, depicts a setting that would become iconic in many later science fiction films.

With the April 22, 1952, telecast of the Nevada test shot Charlie, the mythic terrain of the NTS was brought into the living rooms of millions of Americans.[15] News stories no longer sited bomb tests "outside of Las Vegas" but began to use the names of such specific places as Yucca Flats, Frenchman's Flats, and "News Knob" as Americans became more familiar with the terrain of the test site itself. During the telecast, *New York*

2. Troops march into the darkness cast by a mushroom cloud in Nevada, 1952.

Times reporter and Manhattan Project publicist William Laurence was asked, by a television reporter from KTLA in Los Angeles, "Did they split a little piece of the universe this morning?" Laurence enthusiastically replied, "They did! They did!"[16]

The obsession with arranging a live broadcast of the test and the subsequent heroic efforts by KTLA's general manager, Klaus Landsberg, led to the longest remote pickup that had been attempted by a television crew to that time—277 miles. KTLA gambled with $40,000, six cameras, and thirty-nine technicians over six days and managed to reach an estimated thirty-five million viewers.[17]

Beyond the exposure that such media events brought to the testing program, an equally important facet was being communicated: the look of the desert test site. The crackling black-and-white picture, which faded in and out, showing yuccas and the Joshua trees, excited newsmen, the blast in the desert distance, and crowds of soldiers pitted against this horrific force—all became stock imagery for science fiction films for the rest of the decade. A cultural space was being marked off; the futuristic world of atomic bombs was being broadcast into living rooms in homes across the nation. This setting, which introduced millions of Americans to atomic bombs as a real physical presence in their world, would resonate culturally for all who watched and be imprinted on their memories. The mere sight of the Nevada desert in a science fiction movie would arouse in viewers the expectation that the future was about to unfold before their eyes.

A few very celebrated citizens inhabited the new futuristic landscape of Nuclear Nevada: the mannequin residents of the house at "Elm and Main," who volunteered to go through a nuclear explosion on our behalf.[18] These average American mannequins took up their stations in cars, living rooms, and bomb shelters in a brave attempt to survive an atomic blast. Their story was told far and wide in the American media, since clues to our own potential survival seemed embedded in their experiences.

On March 17, 1953, the United States conducted test shot Annie at the NTS. This test involved extensive participation by civil defense authorities working to measure the effects of the bomb on a wide variety of building materials, clothing, animals, trees, and shelters. This test was open to the media and was widely reported by the press, and reporters dubbed the hastily constructed town the mannequins inhabited "Doom Town." "Two New England–style colonial frame houses, outfitted with surplus government furniture, one sited half a mile from 'ground zero,' the other one and a half miles away," were outfitted with a dozen family bomb shelters, ranging from a simple lean-to any handy man could build for $40 worth of materials to a $100 corner shelter room, able to hold four persons and carry a maximum load of debris; cinder-block and concrete slab rooms ($200); and more elaborate reinforced-concrete shelters costing $1000 and up."[19]

Of the two houses, it was "House One," located 3,500 feet (roughly six city blocks) from ground zero, that became the focus of national attention. An actual street sign was placed in front of the house, marked with the names of Elm and Main. Photographs of House One were reprinted in a wide variety of settings. *Time* ran them on March 30, 1953, and *Nevada Highways and Parks* ran them in its Autumn 1953 issue. A film clip of House One blowing up is among the most widely reproduced pieces of footage from the NTS.[20]

Time grimly reported its fate: three hours after the detonation, the structure was so radioactive that it could not be entered: "House One looked like a match box crumpled on a table. . . . For an area nearly a mile and a half long and almost as wide, the desert had been made dangerous with radioactivity. Hopefully, FCDA [Federal Civil Defense Administration] men announced that the bomb shelters in the cellar of House Two would save real inhabitants."[21]

Nevada Highways and Parks ran a series of eight pictures of the destruction of House One, describing the building as "entirely collapsed and wrecked." The visual image of the house seemed to refer naturally to matchsticks: "Tornadic force tears House Number One asunder like matches," claimed the text accompanying one of the photographs. The image of House One being ripped violently to shreds was indeed a horrific and gripping demonstration of nuclear fury. The images of the frame smoldering from the heat microseconds before the whole structure was ripped apart by the blast were indeed haunting and powerful.[22]

But when the images were printed in the official FCDA pamphlet 2⅔ *Seconds*, civil defense officials found that the story of House One actually carried a message of hope. 2⅔ *Seconds* claimed to present "stop motion pictures of the effects of heat and blast from a 15-kiloton atomic explosion on House No. 1." The 2.66 seconds were broken into 26 individual frames, and the text accompanying frame 26 states grimly, "This once was a house." But there was good news lurking down below. A twenty-seventh image showed a female mannequin, who apparently had gone unharmed through the violent destruction of House One. "HOME SHELTERS CAN SAVE YOU," claimed the final words of the pamphlet: "This mannequin, protected by a basement lean-to shelter, was unharmed."[23] Yet *Time* reported that the house was so radioactive that test workers could not enter it, not commenting on how this fact might affect the mannequins' "survival."

Many American magazines found images of mannequin victims of atomic blasts strangely fascinating (fig. 3). In 1955, *Life* ran an article titled "Victims at Yucca Flats" that showed only the effects of atomic blasts on various mannequins. The descriptions of these lifeless bodies were marked by an obsessive normalization; they became "residents of an entire million-dollar village built to test the effects of an atomic blast on everything from houses to clothes to canned soup." And like the Americans whose places the mannequins took, they came through the tests "disheveled but still haughty on the sands and in the homes of Yucca Flats."[24] Not all the mannequin surrogates were so lucky, however. The *Las Vegas Review-Journal* grieved for a couple of would-be humans: "A mannequin mother died horribly in her one-story house of precast concrete slabs. Portions of her plaster and paint body were found in three different areas. A mannequin tot, perhaps the size of your three-year-old, was blown out of bed and showered with needle-sharp glass fragments."[25]

3. A mannequin family after a nuclear test in Nevada, 1953.

One short year after test shot Annie, Mickey Rooney stumbled his way into the house at Elm and Main in the film *The Atomic Kid*.[26] Rooney plays an aspiring uranium miner who survives an atomic blast in the house, but as a result becomes highly radioactive. Radioactivity lends him strange powers—for example, he can trigger jackpots from Las Vegas slot machines, and he finds that he begins to glow whenever he becomes sexually aroused; eventually, however, the unusual power "goes away." The setting in which he finds himself, a brand-new frame house filled with mannequins, had gained enough ground in mass culture to serve as a popular reference, as it does in this 1954 movie. Nevada was seen as a place in the wide-open West, where America bordered on tomorrow—a perspective that popular culture texts would enthusiastically embrace throughout the remainder of the atmospheric testing era.

Animal Guides to Tomorrow Land

Like travelers in a fairy tale, Americans who began the journey into the atomic age were often taught by animals to navigate this strange new world. Animals functioned as familiars in stories about the atomic future as well as the atomic present. As representatives of nature and the natural response to the new weapons, they helped show humans the appropriate feelings about nuclear weapons, and they channeled information about the new world that we had entered—its dangers, its promises, and its terrors. They began as surrogates sent to encounter atomic bombs on an intimate level we were not prepared to endure ourselves. Stories of their survival fortified us, and they soon became mascots who instructed both our children and ourselves about how to respond to nuclear weapons. But their exposure to radiation would contaminate them and turn them from ally to enemy, although even as adversaries they conveyed critical information about the world we had entered.

The first appearance of animals in atomic history and culture was as participants—or rather, as victims—of nuclear testing.[27] Starting in Bikini Atoll in 1946, tests employed a wide range of creatures in order to gather data about the weapons' effects on living organisms. Operation Crossroads, as the 1946 Bikini tests were officially called, involved the use of 5,664 live animals.[28] Seventy-seven ships were anchored at Bikini for two tests.[29] The first weapon was air-dropped, and the second was detonated under water. According to the official public record of Operation Crossroads, published in 1947, 204 goats, 200 pigs, 200 mice, 60 guinea pigs, and 5,000 rats participated in the two tests.[30] In both cases the animals were held on ships anchored in the lagoon to test their exposure to the blast. The closest to the explosion that any of the 42,000 human participants were stationed was fifteen miles; the animal-laden ships were scattered throughout the blast zone, and even at ground zero.[31]

These animals, like the mannequins, were often dramatically anthropomorphized. Individual species were selected because they approximated human beings in one way or another and would yield data that would be useful about humans. Pigs were chosen specifically for approximating the human body, and lab rats were used because of the similarity of their internal systems and organs to those of humans. Experiments also included testing the flammability of a variety of military uniforms that were tailored to the pigs, and even testing a variety of creams designed to protect the skin from exposure to the flash of a bomb. Rats were obtained from the National Cancer Society, bred for their predilection either to resist or to succumb to cancers.

The animals used in the tests were placed in areas of the ships where, during a war, human personnel might find themselves when a weapon was detonated, including the officers' bathroom.[32] Goats and pigs were also kept in pens on the decks. The press was very interested in the presence of the animals, and after the tests it was declared that only 10 percent of them had died in the blast; but this initial good news gave way in a few short weeks to reports that the Bikini animals were "dying like flies."[33]

The Bikini tests were actually a well-managed public-relations disaster. The real lesson of these tests was the extent of the danger posed by residual radiation: initially, three tests were planned, but the second test—detonation of the underwater bomb—resulted in such high levels of radioactivity in the waters around Bikini that immediate evacuation of all personnel was necessary, and the third test was canceled. The United States was very successful at keeping this fact from becoming widely publicized, leaving the American people thinking about the blast area of the weapon rather than its radioactive perils.

The Bikini animals remained a source of fascination and inspiration for almost a decade. The most famous was Pig 311, which, according to the newspapers, was found swimming in the Bikini lagoon after the first test.[34] In the fall of 1946, both Pig 311 and her fellow celebrity animal survivor, Goat 315, were transferred to the U.S. Navy Medical Research Institute in Bethesda, Maryland, and then to the National Zoo in Washington, D.C..[35] The Smithsonian Institute has a file of "correspondence" between Pig 311 and her admirers. She died in 1950 but came back to life in 1951 as "Patty, the atomic pig" in an article published in *Collier's*, where she told her story in the first person. Patty claimed to have become an admired role model, visited by generals and scientists on the anniversaries of the Bikini test.[36]

In the wake of Russia's development of nuclear weapons at the end of 1949, and during the obsession with surviving a Russian attack that the event fueled, the Bikini animals provided a framework within which people could understand what it took to survive. Richard Gerstell was a civil defense consultant and the author of the first mass-market survival guide, *How to Survive an Atomic Bomb*.[37] In a 1950 *Saturday Evening Post* article about surviving a nuclear attack, he looks to the goats of Bikini for an important lesson:

> Incidentally, some of the goats used in the first Bikini test had previously been sent to Cornell University for a checkup. Several psychoneurotic ones were then selected, so that the scientists would be able to see what effects the nuclear explosion had upon their nervous systems, and in this way perhaps the human susceptibility to crack-up

and panic could be determined. A protected movie camera was focused upon one such goat before the test. When the film was developed later, it showed the goat calmly eating before the detonation. At the moment of explosion there was a mass of flying objects on the screen; and then, this clearing, the goat once more could be seen to be eating calmly and very much undisturbed. No collapse. No nervous breakdown.[38]

The lesson was clear: undue fear of atomic weapons and explosions is irrational.

Animals were used throughout the atmospheric testing era, but following their lead, humans moved closer and closer to ground zero, until the late 1950s, when some were stationed less than four miles from weapon tests.[39] Information about the continued use of animals in nuclear weapons tests was not provided to the press, and as people became more aware of humans on the nuclear horizon the fates of exposed animals became less compelling.

Animals continued to have an important presence in nuclear culture, however, as guides and interpreters of nuclear weapons to human beings. The most famous of these animal guides was Bert the Turtle, who taught children how to survive a nuclear attack. Bert was the mascot of the *Duck and Cover* program of the Federal Civil Defense Administration, appearing in a film, a filmstrip, and pamphlets that were shown and distributed in schools nationwide.[40] Because an atomic attack might happen suddenly, without warning, the campaign was designed to teach children techniques for surviving an attack on their own, without adults to assist them. Bert guided his young audience through these techniques in a variety of settings typical of the life of a child. He taught them always to watch for the flash of a detonation and to duck and cover to avoid the effects of the blast.

The use of animal guides to instruct humans in the proper ways to feel and respond to nuclear weapons extended far beyond the how-to-survive instructions of the civil defense literature. Figure 4, for example, is taken from a book produced by the Atomic Energy Commission (the agency that oversaw all aspects of the development, testing, and production of nuclear weapons) and distributed to members of communities located downwind from the NTS.

This booklet, *Atomic Tests in Nevada*, known as the Green Book because of its kelly-green cover, was designed to ease the fears of the local residents about exposure to radioactive fallout.[41] The picture shows a

4. A downwinder cowboy gazes at a nuclear test as his horse grazes in the Atomic Energy Commission 1955 pamphlet *Atomic Tests in Nevada*.

cowboy on horseback observing a nuclear detonation in Nevada (fig 4). The cowboy represents a member of the downwind community who is considering the mushroom cloud, which has become his neighbor. The horse, however, does not *consider* the explosion; rather, it reacts to it *instinctively*, and the animal's reaction serves as an instruction to the cowboy. The horse doesn't even seem to notice that a nuclear weapon has exploded; like the psychoneurotic goats of Bikini, it does not look up—it keeps on grazing, carefree. The implication is that the horse's reaction to the bomb is the natural one and that the cowboy should take his cue from the horse, so much closer to nature than humans are, and rid himself of any fear or worry about the weapon tests. "Your cooperation has helped achieve an unusual safety record," the Green Book assures readers. "To our knowledge no one outside of the test site has been hurt in six years of testing."[42]

Such iconography was not limited to government publications. In September 1953, children in both public and private schools across America were greeted upon their return to school with a free copy of *Picture Parade* magazine. The cover showed a young boy in the desert, playing

5. A boy and his dog ignore a nuclear explosion on the front cover of a 1953 *Picture Parade.*

with his dog while the mushroom cloud of a nuclear weapon test rises on the horizon behind him (fig. 5).[43]

Even without text, the illustration communicates a great deal of information to the students it addresses. The setting is clearly Nevada: there are cacti, sandy red soil, and other markers of the desert—and of course the mushroom cloud, right behind a mesa. The boy stands in for American children everywhere: his shirt is red-and-white striped, and his pants are a royal blue, giving him the look of someone wearing an American flag above his PF Flyers. But the principal lesson of the picture is the relationship of the boy to the atomic bomb just over his left shoulder. He is oddly at peace with the ominous mushroom cloud.

The boy is not alone on the atomic horizon; he has a dog, an atomic familiar who can help him to understand and feel at home in this new nuclear Nevada. The dog also pays no attention to the nuclear explosion but is completely focused on the boy. Like the horse in the image from the Green Book, the dog's reason for being in the picture is to indicate to the reader the *natural* response to sharing the horizon with a mushroom cloud—to living in a world with nuclear weapons. And the message is the same: Relax and be calm. Act natural. All is well.

In these texts, animals are invoked as atomic familiars who can guide concerned humans through the dangers and fears of the atomic age. "Animals take blasts in stride," asserted a 1953 story about the NTS in *National Geographic*.[44] Stories about animals surviving atomic tests and animals' reactions to atomic explosions were meant to communicate information about what it took for a person to survive in the nuclear future as it unfolded around Americans during the early years of the Cold War, and specifically as it unfolded near the test site. In Patty's case, it was individual courage; in the case of Gerstell's goats, it was calm. These creatures were credited with human characteristics, and tales of their survival provided good news for all who hoped to live through atomic explosions.

But all was not well. There were very real dangers on the atomic horizon, and the presence of animals in the early days of the Cold War was most powerful as a signifier of these dangers. In 1953, the fallout from a test in Nevada resulted in the deaths of 4,200 sheep pastured downwind in Utah.[45] If the animals in the Green Book and *Picture Parade* were meant to instruct readers that there was nothing to fear from nuclear weapons tests, these dead sheep vividly conveyed the message that there might, after all, be something drastic to fear from the fallout clouds. It was not difficult for people living in areas where the sheep had died to imagine that the animals were just one step ahead of them in entering the radioactive future.

It was on movie screens across America that animals took center stage as the harbingers of the dangers of the atomic age. Starting with the giant ants of *Them!* in 1954, animals warned moviegoers about the dangers that accompanied them on their journey into the atomic future. Like Old Testament prophets marching two by two onto Noah's atomic ark, first ants, then octopuses, shrews, Gila monsters, tarantulas, mantises, rats, grasshoppers, rabbits, and scorpions all grew to giant size and called from the silver screen to warn Americans of the dangers of genetic mutation and the destructive power of the new weapons.

Animals were not malicious in these movies: they acted naturally. Human technology, however, had intervened and shifted the balance of nature. Typically, this change agent was represented as radiation, the instrument of human activity, dramatically increasing an animal's size, altering its relationship to its environment. Suddenly, species that had not previously preyed on humans now specifically sought them out to kill or eat, as though to punish us for tampering with the natural order.

In other movies, such as *Tarantula*, a scientist specifically creates giant species of animals in scientific experiments.[46] The scientist is trying to accomplish good—in this case, to develop a means to feed a hungry world—but his efforts end up backfiring and threatening humankind. Such narratives cast doubt on the world of peace and plenty that scientists and elected officials were promising as the end result of the development of nuclear weapons. In fact, in *Tarantula*, a nuclear weapon must be used in order to destroy the giant spider, showing the utility of weapon technology and the futility of the promise of the "peaceful atom."

These movies conveyed warnings about the dangers of genetic mutation as a result of heavy loads of radioactivity entering the environment, in a format that could be easily understood. They were not accurate, in that genetic mutations almost never result in a mutation that retains the original life form but grows to giant proportions, but the message was clear: upsetting the balance of nature is likely to pose a threat to human society. In this way, the animals of the giant bug movies acted as sentinels, urging humans to beware of the dangers they were setting into motion in the natural world by pursuing nuclear technologies.

⇾≋⇽

Animals functioned as atomic familiars in popular culture; they channeled information about the impending future to help us better understand the present. As representatives of nature, they presented the visible
face of the changes that nuclear weaponry thrust upon the world. Whether as harbingers of warning or comfort, animals were the medium used
to signify the natural order, instructing us about the natural place of
atomic weapons and the natural response to them.

2

Fallout Stories

> Martin: How long have you been here?
> Denab: Since the beginning of your experiments in nuclear
>   fission.
> Martin: What have you got to do with that?
> Denab: We are accumulating the energy released with each
>   of your atomic explosions.
>
> *Atomic scientist Dr. Doug Martin and the alien leader*
> *Denab, conversing under the Nevada Test Site in*
> Killers From Space (1954)

Bravo: Putting Fallout on the Map

Nuclear radiation was one of the most potent icons of the atomic age. At first an abstraction associated with the horrors of a nuclear war, during the atmospheric testing era (1945–1963) radiation became a very real part of the lives of Americans, carried into their homes and minds by wind and rain in the form of radioactive fallout from nuclear weapon testing. As testing increased in the 1950s, and as thermonuclear weapons began to be tested, higher and higher levels of fallout reached deeper and deeper into the lives, and bodies, of Americans, and of people all around the world.

Fallout was not discussed in detail in the early rush of articles and books about nuclear weapons after 1945; it forced its way into public consciousness through a series of events that devastated the health of those involved. On November 1, 1952, the first U.S. test of a thermonuclear weapon, or H-bomb (the Mike shot of Operation Ivy, exploding approximately 10 megatons), was carried out on Elugelab Island, in the Pacific Ocean. Elugelab, a tiny island in the Enewetak Atoll in the Marshall Islands, was totally destroyed when the explosion created a crater about one mile in diameter and 175 feet deep at its deepest point. The Mike shot required several buildings to house the cryogenics necessary to cool the thermonuclear fuel to a stable point, weighing a total of 200,000 pounds.[1] The Atomic Energy Commission (AEC) was successful in keeping information about the scale of the test secret from the press and public.

Two years later, on March 1, 1954, the first shot of the Castle series, the Bravo shot, located on Bikini Atoll, tested a cryogenics-less (dry) weapon that weighed only 2,000 pounds and was deliverable from an airplane. The Bravo shot would prove to be so immense that it was impossible to contain information about its destructive power. Whereas the AEC had been able to limit knowledge of the fact that the Mike shot was a test of a hydrogen weapon, the thermonuclear nature of the Bravo shot was apparent to the whole world.[2] Bravo yielded an explosive force of 15 megatons of TNT, a force one thousand times more powerful than existing fission weapons and at least twice as powerful as the weapon's designers had predicted.[3]

Beyond the immense yield of the blast of Bravo, it immediately became apparent that this detonation had produced incredible amounts of radioactive fallout. The U.S. military Joint Task Force 7 (which conducted the tests) saw itself compelled to raise the "permissible" level of exposure for its personnel simply because the participants could not avoid receiving the higher dose.[4] Since staging grounds on nearby atolls had to be abandoned because of high radiation levels, all operations had to be conducted solely from ships, impeding proper procedures. The ships were overcrowded with Task Force personnel who had been evacuated from the atolls.[5] Radiation levels on atolls to the east of Bikini reached such alarming levels that the Task Force evacuated their 264 residents.[6] Many of the islanders (who had been about a hundred miles from Bravo's epicenter) suffered radiation sickness, with such effects as loss of hair and low white blood cell counts, hemorrhages, and skin lesions.[7] The New York Times carried its first article about the exposure of the islanders on March 12, 1954.[8]

Two days later, a Japanese tuna trawler, known as the Fukuryu Maru (Lucky Dragon), pulled into its slip in the Japanese port town of Yaizu. On the day of the test the ship had been at anchor over ninety miles east of ground zero (well outside the fifty-mile exclusion zone set up by the Joint Task Force), yet it had been exposed to very heavy amounts of fallout from the test. All twenty-three members of the crew were ill, and one later died from radiation exposure.[9]

The Bravo test, with its terrible toll on human life and health, marked the end of the successful containment of the issue of radioactive fallout that the U.S. government had been able to maintain for the first nine years of the atomic age. Throughout its coverage of the Bravo incident in the spring of 1954, the New York Times still put the word fall-out in quotation marks. Prior to the Bravo test, fallout, when mentioned in the press, was generally referred to as "residual" or "lingering" radiation.

The first article to mention radioactive fallout inside the United States was a report of downwind fallout from the Trinity test in New Mexico in July 1945. *Newsweek* ran a short piece on November 12 of that year reporting that "mysterious radioactivity was affecting photographic film at an Eastman Kodak plant." The article explained that the film had been affected by "radioactive strawboard" used to make shipping boxes. The boxes used "straw cut in Illinois on Aug. 6, just 21 days after the explosion of the first atomic bomb in New Mexico" (no mention is made of the fact that this was also the day Hiroshima was bombed), and "radioactive residues" had "fallen" on the field of straw.[10]

The American public again encountered the idea of dangerous levels of radioactive fallout after the Bikini tests in 1946. David Bradley's influential 1948 record of Operation Crossroads, *No Place to Hide*, was essentially a book about fallout. "What happened at Crossroads was the clearest measure yet of the menace of atomic energy," Bradley wrote. "Less spectacular perhaps than Hiroshima and Nagasaki, the Bikini tests give a far clearer warning of the lingering and insidious nature of the radioactive agent that makes it such an ideal weapon for use on civil populations."[11] This perspective echoed more official pronouncements: Admiral William Blandy, the head of the Joint Task Force that conducted the tests, was quoted in *Time* two weeks after testing had concluded with the single phrase, "It's a poison weapon." A picture below the quote showed sailors trying to scrub radioactivity from an Operations Crossroads ship, which remained contaminated. *Time* compared the tenacious radioactivity to "the blood on Bluebeard's key."[12]

Bradley, a physician who was a radiological monitor for Operation Crossroads, described a medical decision he was confronted with weeks after the blast. A sailor in his late teens was sent to see Bradley because he had been cut by a piece of radioactive cable. "The sailor told us the name of the ship; it was one of the beached vessels and was moderately contaminated on deck. . . . 'I was heaving in on one of the cables when it broke and tore my hand. Don't seem too bad, but one of the Geiger men was there and he sent me right over here.'" Bradley explained to the sailor that "in laboratories and plants where people are working with purified plutonium there is a policy which requires immediate high amputation for anyone in a similar situation." The sailor solemnly nodded and said, "You're the doctor." This harrowing incident painted a grim picture of "lingering" radiation as capable of contaminating a person long after a nuclear explosion, and made clear that the contamination was dangerous enough to require removing a limb to stave off the possibility of a more severe fate.[13]

Radioactive contamination claimed more than ships at Bikini and limbs from servicemen. *Time* reported in 1947 that "at one university, two entire buildings have been so radioactivated that they can no longer be used for atomic work; at another center, a researcher in one afternoon infected a laboratory so badly that the walls had to be taken down and replaced."[14] Radiation seemed infectious, insidious, and persistent.

In the frenzy following the first Soviet nuclear weapon test in late 1949, military speculation about the possible use of radiological poisons as a weapon separate from the use of actual nuclear weapons began to find expression in the popular press. "An invisible dust of radioactive 'death sand' could spread over cities of the earth and kill their populations by radioactivity without the noisy warning of an atomic bomb," according to the *Science News-Letter*. Leaving nothing to the imagination, the article explained that "very fine sand would be coated with these radioactive poisons and spread very thinly over the area where it is desired to wipe out life." That same week *Time* reported that "less than a ton of death sand, evenly distributed, would make Manhattan a deathtrap."[15]

Such speculation was fairly rare before 1954, but the Bravo test put fallout on the map, and in the years immediately after the test thousands of articles a year would appear with the word *fallout* in the title. The test itself was a source of mysterious and powerful stories. "Whether the public should be told the truth about the devastating fall-out from the H-bomb explosions is the subject of a bitter behind-the-scenes argument between the AEC and the Civil Defense Administration," *Newsweek* reported in "The Inside Story" on November 8, 1954. "One estimate now is that the H-bomb tested last March at [Elugelab] rendered uninhabitable an elliptical area of 4,000 square miles—nearly the size of Connecticut—downwind from the blast."[16]

The scale of the Bravo fallout was told in personal terms in the *Saturday Evening Post* in July 1957, in a story titled "We Were Trapped by Radioactive Fallout" by Dr. John C. Clark, the commander of the firing party for the Bravo test. He and eight others in the sand-covered control bunker for the test, about a dozen miles away from ground zero, had to take shelter for around twelve hours in a small communications room in the bunker when, soon after the blast, radiation readings in the main room spiked to dangerously high levels.

Radiation levels outside of the bunker were substantially higher still, so the men were unable to escape, since no ship or helicopter could come close—in fact, they were all in the process of moving further back because of the fallout. The men in the bunker determined that the tiny communications room had the lowest level of radioactivity, and they barricaded themselves in to wait for the levels to fall sufficiently to execute a rescue. "We were not exactly a happy bunch as we sat around in that small back room. We had been forced to turn off the air conditioner because it brought in fallout particles from outside. The entire building soon got hot and sticky." A little over an hour later, "our generator began failing and the lights gradually went out, leaving us in darkness." This was around 8:00 in the morning—help finally arrived at 5:30 in the afternoon. The men came out of the communications room to determine if the radiation level outside had made it safe enough to dash to a rescue helicopter. Clark added the ghostly detail that when they were finally able to run the helicopters, "to keep the 'hot' dust off of our bodies, we wrapped ourselves completely in bed sheets, cutting holes only for our eyes." The next day, Clark writes, they found out that the radiation levels just outside their bunker had been lethal.[17]

While many AEC-friendly articles dismissed the danger of fallout in the mid-1950s, there were countless references to fallout as unspeakably dangerous. It was referred to as "the ultra-modern horror, radioactive smog," and as "fantastically poisonous radioactivity."[18] The story of how fallout was impacting the people who lived downwind from the Nevada Test Site was broken open by journalist Paul Jacobs in his seminal article, "Clouds from Nevada," published in the *Reporter* in May 1957. Jacobs's article told of cancers and other deadly health problems becoming endemic among the downwinders. He told of seven-year-old Martin Bardolini dying of leukemia as a result of exposure to fallout, of people who had lost their hair, and of the residents of St. George, Utah, who had been "continuously exposed for sixteen days to atmospheric contamination." He wrote about massive die-offs of sheep and cattle after fallout clouds from nuclear tests had passed over their grazing lands, and of "bead-like particles" of fallout raining down on local ranches.[19]

By the mid-1950s, "residual" and "lingering" radiation had given way to almost universal use of the word *fallout*. Maps were printed in magazines and newspapers showing the paths of fallout clouds from tests in Nevada over the continental United States. The Bravo test had opened the eyes of Americans to the dangers of nuclear testing, and how radioactive their world was becoming. What they would see with these new eyes would very much surprise them.

Behind the Radioactive Curtain: Monsters and Aliens

Surrounded by army troops aiming flamethrowers into the burning egg chamber where the last of the terrifying giant ants lay dying, the heroes of the 1954 movie *Them!* considered the origin of the mutants: "If those monsters got started as a result of the first atomic bomb test in 1945, what about all of the others that have been exploded since then?"[20] This question, expressing Americans' anxiety about atomic testing during the mid-1950s, was to be answered in abundance by Hollywood filmmakers.[21]

Between 1945 and 1965, over five hundred science fiction films, many depicting threats as bizarre as the giant ants, were released to the theatergoing public.[22] On film, the atomic age was filled with overgrown monsters and invading aliens, and radiation was the catalyzing element that legitimized the birth into our world of evil and destructive forces. Whether these threats materialized as monsters generated or regenerated from beneath the ocean, the desert, or the polar icecaps, or as extraterrestrials who sought to destroy the earth, radiation functioned as their life-giving source: the threat either was born out of radiation or was feeding off it. Atomic test sites, nuclear power plants, and atomic labs were common science fiction movie settings.

Atomic monsters of the 1950s, having passed through a baptism of radiation, possessed a license to terrorize and were resistant to conventional military weapons. Two types of cinematic monsters were used to typify the threat: those portrayed in films like *Godzilla*, in which dormant primordial threats were reawakened, often by the testing of an atomic bomb, and the products of genetic mutation in nature, brought about by radiation from earlier atomic tests, which typically resulted in a monstrous and unnatural threat to the human race from some other species; these are know as the "giant bug" movies. The first type, the primordial monsters, usually targeted cities, while the giant bugs tended to stay close to atomic facilities. Both of the specific examples I mentioned earlier, *Them!* and *Godzilla*, were released in 1954, following the publicity from the Bravo test and its subsequent radioactive contamination of islanders, fisherman, and servicemen.

Ishiro Honda made the classic film *Gojira* in Japan; it was released in the fall of 1954.[23] The American director Terrell O. Morse later shot separate footage of the actor Raymond Burr, which was spliced into an edited version of the Japanese original, and this version was released in the United States in April 1956 as *Godzilla, King of the Monsters!*[24] An H-bomb test was the event that freed Godzilla from the ocean floor. The first hint that something monstrous is afoot is a Japanese fishing boat that bursts into flames on the high seas and sinks; the use of this image just after the tragedy of the *Fukuryu Maru* occurred in Japan was, according to Honda, deliberate.[25] Godzilla, an ancient dinosaurlike monster, emerges from the water and eventually trashes most of Tokyo. Godzilla emits radioactive fire-breath, and so, as he stomps through Tokyo, he blazes a radioactive trail, burning Japanese boats and torching buildings just as real bombs do. The scenes that depict Tokyo after the destruction refer both to the nuclear devastation of Hiroshima and Nagasaki and the 1945 firebombing of Tokyo and every other Japanese city with a population in excess of 50,000. The sudden presence of this monster is legitimized by its birth in an atomic explosion; no further explanation is necessary.

In *The Beast from 20,000 Fathoms* (1953), a dinosaur frozen under the North Pole is thawed out by an atomic test, freeing it to swim along the coast and attack New York City. In *It Came from Beneath the Sea* (1953), an octopus is made radioactive after an H-bomb test, grows to giant size, and strikes San Francisco.[26] Each of these monsters is made to go through an atomic rebirth in order to regenerate into this world and threaten its cities, and in each case this rebirth is the result of weapons testing, not the general destruction of a full-scale nuclear war. This plot device highlights the growing fears of Americans (and Japanese) of radioactive contamination during this period of intensive atmospheric testing—fears both connected to and separate from fears of an actual nuclear attack.

The first and most successful of the giant bug movies was *Them!* Released in June 1954, it hit theaters just after the newspapers were full of stories about radioactive fish from the Bravo test and the sickness of the *Fukuryu Maru* crew and the Pacific islanders.[27] *Them!* is the story of a giant ant colony that forms on the desert floor at the Trinity site as a result of the radiation unleashed by that first atomic test. The giant ants, which Spencer Weart describes as "the size of buses," have to be destroyed at any cost; their very existence threatens all humankind.[28] Intriguingly, although much of *Them!* takes place in New Mexico, the desert sets are filled with Joshua trees, which do not grow in New Mexico but are native to the area of the Nevada Test Site.

The giant ants are not in themselves evil; rather it is merely that when normal ant behavior is enlarged on such a monstrous scale, the change upsets the balance of nature, ultimately threatening human society. This theme is true of almost all the giant bug movies, such as *Tarantula*, *The Deadly Mantis*, and *The Black Scorpion*.[29] Because of their radioactive birth, these monsters are inherently stronger and more deadly than they were in their pre-mutant form, and this unnatural strength and size makes their normal behavior unnaturally violent. While monsters like Godzilla represent a regeneration of primordial forces of destruction, the giant ants of *Them!* represent the birth of a new and modern form of monster: a future monster, one that represents a manmade shift in the natural balance.

Among the most powerful indictments of our own knowledge of atomic energy was the 1958 Canadian movie *The Fiend Without a Face*. Here the monsters that threaten human society are our own brains. The threat originates in the mind of Professor Walgate, a scientist. Attempting to move objects with his mind, Walgate succeeds when his equipment is struck by lightning. This burst of energy allows his thought to take on existence independent of his brain. This individuated thought begins to tap into the permanent energy of an "atomic pile" that powers a nearby "atomic radar" station. Soon hundreds, if not thousands, of these thoughts have taken form by using atomic power as an energy source. The monsters, invisible through most of the film, begin to kill the local residents. The manner in which they kill is particularly instructive: they suck out their victims' brains and spinal cords through two puncture wounds at the base of the skull; one of the townsfolk describes them as "mental vampires." The invisible monsters increase the energy output from the pile, "feeding," as it were, and become visible: they are brains attached to spinal cords, which they use to propel themselves like inchworms. Under siege by thousands of these monsters, the military heroes of the film blow up the pile's control room, killing the faceless fiends.[30]

The symbolism of the movie is boldly condemning of even the knowledge of atomic energy: the monsters that threaten society are actually the thoughts of scientists, in the physical form of brains. These thoughts directly feed on atomic energy to exist, gain power, and kill, and they are given a destructive ability that is *independent* of the will of the scientist in whose head they originate. The movie's message is simple: atomic-powered scientific thought is monstrous and evil. Our brains have become our own worst enemies.

For alien invaders in popular culture texts, radiation often functions as the marker of an access-point to the earth. Alien invasions frequently set up home bases near atomic facilities. Often it is these same facilities that are the targets of the invasion, the aliens somehow being desperate for new sources of power or even desperate to kidnap atomic scientists for their prized specialized knowledge.[31]

Whether it is atomic energy or weapons that gives these monsters or aliens authority to enter our world, the Nevada desert is their point of entry. In *Killers from Space* (1954), alien invaders have set up shop in caves beneath the Nevada Test Site and are feeding off of the energy released by each bomb blast. They use this energy, and the energy from an attached atomic-power generating station, to grow gigantic bugs and animals, which they intend to set loose in order to take over the planet. These aliens resurrect an atomic scientist (played by Peter Graves), whose plane they have caused to crash immediately following an atomic test because they are desperate to obtain his knowledge about upcoming tests. Eventually the scientist destroys the aliens and their giant mutant army by cutting the power flow from the atomic plant for ten seconds. This interruption causes the aliens' base to explode in a nuclear blast, complete with mushroom cloud (borrowed from film of the second Bikini test).

In *This Island Earth* (1955), nuclear scientists are again the targets of invading aliens, who are in need of experts to help them refuel their dying planet. Targeted scientists are first contacted by being sent the schematics to a sophisticated device that can communicate and transport matter. Once they have constructed the device, the aliens begin to communicate with them and enlist their help. In this instance, the natural technological curiosity of the nuclear scientists provides an entry point to admit alien forces into this world.[32]

In futurist fiction, aliens who threaten to take over the earth because of their need for atomic power were invited here because we had crossed the nuclear threshold. Rather than liberating us, our achievement of this level of power has made us the target of intergalactic violence. Atomic power and weapons have opened a doorway through which terrors from far-off worlds are given license to destroy us. These aliens were invariably portrayed as technologically more sophisticated extensions of ourselves: they, too, relied on violence to achieve their goals.

All such conjectures seemed *natural* because by the mid-1950s the Nevada desert had become a mythic zone where supernatural events could be *expected* to happen. In *The Amazing Colossal Man* (1957), a man who walks onto the Nevada Test Site just as a "plutonium bomb" is being tested becomes a giant and then attacks Las Vegas.[33] In *Attack of the 50-Foot Woman* (1957), a woman is turned into a giant by an alien whom she meets in the Nevada desert.[34] Many of these movies, such as *Killers from Space*, begin with a shot that pans across the desert landscape, always showing the Joshua trees that had come to symbolize the test site. To Americans in theaters everywhere, the image of a Joshua tree silhouetted in the Nevada desert had become a cultural marker announcing that the supernatural was just around the corner.

Cold War Equivalency: Political Fallout in Popular Culture

Because of the unique characteristics and radical new dangers of nuclear weapons, nuclear icons played a fascinating part in fueling a political critique of the Cold War that was expressed in the coded language of popular culture. Science fiction narratives, both in fiction and in film, pioneered this use of popular culture texts as effective tools for criticizing the Cold War, presenting ideas that could not be safely expressed in more mainstream channels of culture and discourse.

One of the most subversive political perspectives subtly expressed through popular culture was the idea that there was no difference between the United States and the Soviet Union: both could be seen as belligerent superpowers. From this perspective, the bullying of smaller countries into bipolar "blocs" and the commitment of the wealth of both societies to an endless arms race made the two opponents seem to be almost interchangeable.

While scientists and politicians would have put themselves in danger had they openly articulated such a critique, Americans accepted the idea when they found it expressed in the popular 1951 science fiction film *The Day the Earth Stood Still*.[35] Often described as a Christian allegory, in which the peaceful and Christ-like Klaatu (who takes the earthly name Mr. Carpenter) descends from the heavens to deliver the new law of nonviolence to the barely mature earthlings, *The Day the Earth Stood Still* contained radical messages folded into the very structure of the narrative.[36] Klaatu sees only a brutish and violent species; when he looks at us the differences so essential to Cold War bilateralism are absent. In a telling scene, the American president's chief of staff, who visits Klaatu in the hospital after he is wounded (Klaatu did favor the United States by landing in Washington, D.C.), asks the alien why he has come to the earth. Klaatu explains that his message is for the leaders of all the nations of the world and that they must gather the following day in order to receive it. The American shrugs: "I'm afraid that given our present political situation, that is quite impossible." He is, of course, referring to the tensions of the Cold War, which in 1951 made an easily convened meeting of Stalin and Truman unthinkable. Klaatu seems mildly amused. "I do not care about your petty political squabbles," he chides. To characterize the Cold War as a petty political squabble was a radical critique. Klaatu informs the human race that those beings living on other planets had no interest in humans so long as they remained technologically unsophisticated. But since they have now developed nuclear weapons and are therefore a threat to other planets, they are being included in an intergalactic peacekeeping program in which giant robots will destroy any planet that continues to manufacture nuclear weapons. Klaatu shows us that in a world armed with nuclear weapons, all people, regardless of nationality, share a single, common destiny.

The Day the Earth Stood Still expresses a leftist assessment of the Cold War, in which the violence of human society is the enemy of all beings, earthborn or not; but critiques of this sort were by no means limited to the left. The 1952 B-movie *Red Planet Mars* expressed a right-of-center critique of the Cold War that equally demonized both communism and capitalism, the Soviets and the Americans.[37] In *Red Planet Mars*, an American scientist (the ubiquitous Peter Graves) receives radio signals from Mars; these are also intercepted by a corrupt Soviet scientist. The messages, at first aimed at the United States, have the effect of completely undermining capitalism by suggesting that Mars is a planet of abundant energy and food. Declaring that these technologies can easily be transferred to Earth, the messages cause the bottom to drop out of the energy and food markets. The American economy goes into a tailspin, and the film draws the audience along with the suspicion that perhaps the messages are coming from the evil Soviet scientist. Suddenly, the Soviet Union receives messages that question the atheist nature of its society. These messages are phrased as though they were coming directly from God. The effect on Soviet society is to cause the citizens to rise up against their communist leaders and reestablish the Russian Orthodox Church. In the end, the Soviet scientist tries to convince the American scientist that he was the source of all of the messages and that he hates both societies. But as they all die together in the climactic final scene—a fire set by the Soviet scientist in his lab—a further message arrives, confirming that God was the source of the emissions all along.

While both films use Christianity as a vehicle for critiquing the Cold War, it is also important to note that both use science fiction to articulate that opinion. Science fiction, with its inherent suspension of the rules of the real world, allowed the audiences of these films to gain a perspective on the world of the Cold War, one that they could not otherwise easily have found in mass culture. It allowed Americans to step back and see their moment in history from a "big-picture" vantage point, recognizing problems they had previously been too caught up in to see clearly.

The early 1960s gave children a hint at the equivalence of the United States and the Soviet Union in the comic strip "Spy vs. Spy," drawn by Antonio Prohias, which ran in *Mad* magazine. The black spy and the white spy, an obvious reference to the dualism of the Cold War, were neither good nor bad. They were exactly the same—they were interchangeable.[38]

The notion that the United States and the Soviet Union were equivalent was based on the belief that it was the will toward violence that was the real enemy; this feeling was often expressed in the social-science critique of the Cold War discussed in chapter 3. But while social scientists debated ways to understand and eradicate this human tendency, popular culture drew it out to its logical conclusions, so that the characteristic itself could be instructive to the viewer without the attendant violence of the actions. In this manner, popular culture was able to criticize the pathologies of nuclear war without feeling compelled to transform them. Similarly, much of the science fiction of the early Cold War period that is set in the distant future portrayed the earth as a unified planet with a single government, accomplishing in fiction what seemed impossible to accomplish politically.[39]

Critiques of the Cold War were not exclusive to science fiction texts—they were also found in literature produced by leftists and those opposed to nuclear weapons—but science fiction movies and novels had the unique ability to reach a far larger audience across a much broader spectrum of society, including children.[40] With the advent of nuclear weaponry, science fiction had come to play an essential and informing role in American political culture.

≡≒

Popular culture in a nuclear age provided a glimpse behind the veil of the atomic future: an Alice-in-Wonderland venture beyond the present reality and into the radioactive landscape. Radiation became a favorite plot element in popular culture texts that embodied the complex contradictions of the atomic age. In plot or setting, radiation legitimized breaks in normality. This talismanic quality of separating normal from supernatural space or time reflects both aspects of radiation's physical nature (the invisible ability to transmute one element to another and the ability to effect action at a distance), and aspects of its effect on society (marking a potential end time or a golden era of peace and plenty). As nuclear weapons tests moved underground in 1963, so too did the heightened public awareness of radiation, and it became less frequently invoked in popular culture. But just like the cloud that Scott Thomas rose to consider from the deck of his boat in *The Incredible Shrinking Man*, the actual dangers were not really gone, just once again imperceptible to the senses.

It was a uniquely postmodern world that unfolded every day; at the same time that fallout was killing the sheep of downwind ranchers in Nevada and Utah by the thousands, moviegoers across America could watch aliens, intent on destroying humanity, breeding and raising hordes of giant bugs and reptiles underneath the Nevada desert.[41] Wearing 3-D glasses and striding boldly into the future, Americans seemed as ready to explore this land of tomorrow as they had been to fund its creation with their tax dollars. As Americans got into their cars and headed westward to take the kids to Disneyland, radioactive clouds left Nevada and drifted eastward, seeding the future with monsters and mutants and mystery.

3

Nuclear Approach/Avoidance: Social Scientists and the Bomb

The real problem is in the hearts of men.

Albert Einstein

Social Scientists as First Responders to the Atomic Dilemma

As the radioactive mushroom clouds from the atomic bombings of Hiroshima and Nagasaki began to drift across the Pacific Ocean, concerns about the future of human society were already in the air. On August 10, 1945, radio station WNEW in New York ran a special program titled "The Atomic Bomb—The End or Rebirth of Civilization?" In the presentation, the sociologist Harvey Zorbaugh made a powerful and insightful plea to the listeners: "The problem we face is this: During the years we must wait for science to harvest atomic energy in the interests of civilization, can we prevent atomic energy from destroying civilization? . . . There were physicists who predicted that the splitting of the atom would cause the disintegration of the physical universe. The atom has been split and the physical universe maintains its stability. It is the social universe the stability of which has been threatened. The prevention of the disintegration of the social universe is the fateful challenge the Atomic Age throws down to our generation."[1]

In the days immediately following the bombings of Hiroshima and Nagasaki, anxiety about the nature of human beings was voiced throughout American society, and one segment that heard those calls loud and clear and hurried to respond was the social-science community. If human culture needed to be transformed, social scientists claimed, they had the expertise and training to midwife the transformation.

Social scientists felt the same visceral threat to human society that many people sensed in those first days of the atomic age. The world had endured two global wars in thirty years, and these had claimed the lives of more than seventy million people. The violence inherent in human beings and societies seemed only too evident, and the prospect of those violent impulses armed with nuclear weapons was chilling. Many in the social-science community felt called to intervene in this dangerous dynamic.

The historian Paul Boyer has astutely pointed out that "many social scientists in this post-Hiroshima period embraced the view that they possessed knowledge and expertise essential to mankind's survival."[2] This feeling was not merely born out of the urgency accompanying the advent of nuclear weaponry but was also rooted in Progressive-era beliefs that experts could intervene in society to improve seemingly intractable problems, such as poverty and alcoholism. This combination of a global threat to human society, controlled from within the dark recesses of the human personality, and faith in social betterment perfectly challenged the emerging skills of the social-science community in postwar America.

The belief that a social leap forward was needed to avoid global atomic destruction was rooted in anxiety over the impact of technology on American society—a central concern for many social thinkers. At the time of the Hiroshima explosion, the specific question of a gap between technology and society had already provided a prominent career for one sociologist: William Fielding Ogburn of the University of Chicago, an expert who published widely on the social effects of technology. In 1922, Ogburn had first articulated his theory of "cultural lag." He presented a formula for the predicament in which modern society found itself: "Cultural lag occurs when one of two parts of culture which are correlated changes before or in greater degree than the other part does, thereby causing less adjustment between the two parts than existed previously."[3]

Immediately after Hiroshima, Ogburn was widely consulted on the atomic dilemma. In the first days of the atomic age, he was asked to appear on Chicago-area radio stations and to participate in University of Chicago forums to discuss the bomb's impact on society. Ogburn argued that major funding should be secured that would allow expert social scientists to map a successful path to the future.[4]

Ogburn made his case to President Harry Truman; in a letter dated October 1, 1945, he stressed that the bomb's "social effects cannot be well anticipated by natural scientists, but can be predicted and plans made much better by social scientists." He went on to lecture the president: "It is the job of natural scientists to make the discovery, and that of the social scientists to tell what its social consequences will be."[5]

During the same fall, Ogburn testified before a subcommittee of the Senate Committee on Military Affairs in support of additional funds for the social sciences to be included in the annual National Science Foundation bill. In a statement read to the committee, Ogburn laid claim to the social sciences' due: "If money is given to support research in nuclear physics and from this research there come great discoveries which will produce numerous social problems, then it would seem that we should also give money to the social sciences to support study of these problems caused by the researches in nuclear physics." Ogburn concluded wryly that "the alternative of doing nothing or of advising without the benefit of such researches is not very attractive."[6]

Many prominent intellectuals were right behind Ogburn. In *Modern Man Is Obsolete*, Norman Cousins echoed Ogburn's analysis of the predicament: "[Man] has leaped centuries ahead in inventing a new world to live in, but he knows little or nothing about his own part in that world. He has surrounded and confounded himself with gaps—gaps between revolutionary technology and evolutionary man, between cosmic gadgets and human wisdom, between intellect and conscience."[7] George F. Zook, the chairman of President Truman's Commission on Higher Education, also concluded that the world's precarious situation had arisen "largely because discovery in natural science has raced so far ahead of discovery in social science and human behavior."[8]

Lewis Mumford, one of the most articulate critics of technology and defenders of traditional—or, in his own term, "organic"—human forms of society, embraced Ogburn's concept of cultural lag in the atomic age but worried about the length of the lag in this particular case. Writing in 1948, Mumford feared that the time between the advent of atomic weapons and society's ability to control them could not be shortened sufficiently to keep society from being destroyed: "The first full-scale use of the atomic bomb . . . cast a doubt on the whole process to which we have so wholeheartedly committed our civilization. . . . [T]o turn such an instrument loose on society, without erecting fresh moral safeguards and controls, in particular without creating an effective system of world government, was an act of social irresponsibility."[9] For Mumford, a more fundamental change was required than simply increasing institutional support for social-science academics: "Man's principal task today is to create a new self, adequate to command the forces that now operate so aimlessly and yet so compulsively. . . . In short, the moment for another great historic transformation has come."[10] Understandably, Mumford did not look to Congress to fund such an endeavor.

Addressing an audience at the University of Michigan in 1947, the University of Chicago sociologist Louis Wirth, president-elect of the American Sociological Society, called attention to the interdependence of physical sciences and the social sciences in the modern world: "Ever since the days when the people of the world heard the startling announcement of the destruction of a Japanese city by means of the first atomic bomb used in the history of warfare, a new bond of fraternity has been welded between the physical sciences and the social sciences. Never before has the responsibility resting on social science for dealing with the impact of science upon society been as great."[11]

Wirth placed the destiny of human culture squarely on increased funding for the social sciences. "No one can give the assurance that with adequate support and a favorable atmosphere social sciences will succeed in coping with the impact of science and technology in time to prevent the destruction of civilized life on earth," he admitted, but clearly without such funding there was little hope. "The knowledge requisite to the building of a world community and a world government, to mention only one aspect of the social situation created by the discovery of atomic fission, has become indispensable for the survival of civilization."[12]

Hornell Hart, a sociologist at Duke University, agreed with Wirth's pessimistic assessment and with his hope in the culture-saving role destined to be played by social scientists: "Conceivably, social science might be applied to the problem of directing international co-operation toward the protection of mankind from destruction by physical science applied to military technology. If social scientists cannot now begin to grapple effectively with that problem, their life span on this earth seems likely to be severely limited in the near future."[13] Feliks Gross, of Brooklyn College, worried that "in the realm of social interaction, discovery of new destructive energies calls for a much greater organization of human cooperation in various forms and the elimination of conflicts. This is a matter of survival."[14] David Bradley, whose best-selling book on the 1946 nuclear tests at Bikini Atoll was among the first public warnings of the dangers of radioactive fallout, was more direct: "For their own protection [the public] will have to match natural laws with civil laws. Science and sociology are as inseparable now as man and his shadow."[15]

This rhetoric of the need for social transformation as a response to the bomb echoed widely in American society. As early as 1945, Robert Maynard Hutchins, the chancellor of the University of Chicago, advocated reorganizing American universities to focus on educating the public in the values of global citizenship. "We do not know what education can do for us, because we have never tried it. We must try it now. . . . [T]he task is overwhelming, and the chance of success is slight. We must take that chance or die."[16] In 1947, he further advised that those living in free societies "should try to discover the human law which will embrace and bind all members of the human community," claiming that there was no other solution to the threat of atomic weapons.[17]

As Paul Boyer has pointed out, not everyone in the social-science community supported the idea that investment in sociological research was the best road to accomplishing social change; the University of Illinois sociologist Donald R. Taft deemed Ogburn's proposed research projects an example of the cultural lag that Ogburn himself had described. Taft favored the approach of the physicists and chemists that would become known as the scientists' movement, which was marked by political activism and direct appeals to the public. This trend is noted by Boyer, who writes that Ogburn's "business-as-usual academic response to the bomb compared unfavorably to the social activism of the atomic scientists."[18] The *Science News-Letter* advised psychiatrists in December 1945 that "doctors . . . may have to come out of the their offices and hospitals to study the world in which their patients live, following the example of the atomic physicists."[19]

These efforts to advocate for funding and for the importance of the social sciences came directly as a result of the high levels of funding granted social scientists during the war and their successful achievements. While Taft chided the institutional approach of Ogburn and others in their quest for funding in 1945 and 1946, the same criticism could be leveled at social scientists' subsequent efforts to define the nature of the human aspects of the atomic dilemma: a well-stated case by the physical scientists was then followed with badly articulated details on the part of the social scientists. In this case, the atomic scientists would argue that human nature made it essential to place political control over nuclear weapons in international hands, while the social scientists would assert that what was essential was a detailed analysis of the roots of human violent tendencies.

Putting the Human Race on the Couch

The need to address the violence inherent in human nature as a means of working toward avoiding nuclear war was a conceptual framework generally accepted among social scientists. This violence was to be analyzed at two key points of dysfunction: the individual and the nation. In the individual, violent human nature led to aggressive, antisocial behavior; in the nation-state, it led to "nationalism" and warfare. It was convenient to interpret war as a collective expression of individual aggressiveness and violence.

Social-science leaders championed this perspective enthusiastically in the immediate aftermath of Hiroshima, both in professional journals and in the halls of government. "Atomic energy has become a psychological problem," the psychologist David Krech announced in a statement titled "Psychology and Atomic Energy," issued by the Committee on International Peace of the Society for the Psychological Study of Social Issues (SPSSI) and read into the *Congressional Record* on June 12, 1946. "We must see the importance of our own psychology, our own way of thinking, for preventing war and controlling atomic energy. No cannon, no airplane, no atomic bomb can declare war. Only man can do that. The atomic bomb has not plunged the world into an area of the dark and fearful unknown—man's *psychology* is doing that."[20]

The presumption prevailed that social violence was rooted in violent human nature; the very same forces that would drive a psychotic to violent outbursts led societies into warfare. In 1949 Watson Davis, the director of the Science Clubs of America and of the Science Service news agency, told an audience that "disordered and mentally warped personalities give rise to crime of all sorts, including those against society." This diagnosis of antisocial behavior had been accepted since the early days of psychiatry, and the great changes in the atomic age had not altered this fundamental analysis. "Hatred," Davis claimed, "like neurons from fissionable material, can cause emotional chain reactions of great violence." Indeed, Davis advised that it was hatred, not nuclear weaponry, that was the real threat: "As with the atomic bomb, it is already very, very late to try to stop or control these emotional explosions that set peoples against peoples. Despite all the marvelous chemical, medical, engineering and other scientific achievements, the control of the human factor in our civilization constitutes the greatest of our unsolved problems of science."[21]

Many social leaders warned that nuclear weapons presented the human race with a choice between utter destruction brought about by nuclear warfare and the elimination of war itself as a means of solving international conflicts. This choice seemed immediately evident in the aftermath of Hiroshima and Nagasaki. Writing in August 1945, Bruce Bliven, the editor of the *New Republic*, told his readers that "at last it seems literally true that humanity as a whole must either learn to live at peace or face destruction on a grotesquely vast scale." He bleakly concluded, "Candor compels us to admit that nothing in the history of humankind justifies the hope that we shall be able to master this new weapon and exploit its possibilities for good and not for evil."[22]

One week later, Bliven again cautioned that the choice between peace and war was made on the battleground of the human self: "We must

6. A 1945 editorial cartoon considers the implications of the atomic bomb.

understand that both our fears and our hopes are centered not about the material forces of the universe, but about ourselves. The explosive energies of the human personality are far greater than those of the atom, and can have a more devastating effect if released the wrong way."[23] Clearly, if the end of the world were to be avoided, it would be because of the intelligent harnessing of the violent power of human nature (fig. 6).

Such violence was seen as so deeply rooted in human nature that even the promises of a world without war or want that some envisioned in the early days of the atomic age could not offset this drive. The University of Illinois psychiatrist Franz Alexander wrote in 1949, "Theoretically, the mastery of the almost inexhaustible source of atomic energy should give man a greater feeling of security and enable him to lessen the struggle for existence, make him independent of exhaustible resources, reduce his need to subjugate and exploit others." But this promise was an intellectual abstraction when confronted with the depth of human aggressiveness: "His first reaction, however, is to utilize this new source of power for destruction."[24]

Typical of the hastily proposed research plans of the era was the short-lived Manhattan Security Project, spearheaded by the psychologist Goodwin Watson and the anthropologist Theresa Durlach, which met primarily in New York during 1946 and 1947. Watson was a founder and the first president of the SPSSI (which became a division of the American Psychological Association in 1936). The society began publishing the *Journal of Social Issues* in 1945; in 1947, Watson also became the founding editor of the *Journal of Applied Behavioral Sciences*. His earlier activism had resulted in his being called before the House Un-American Activities Committee during World War II. Ian Nicholson has written that "Watson attempted to bring a new, intellectually audacious and politically enlightened 'orientation' to American psychology."[25]

The research plan of the Manhattan Security Project called for it to be "comparable in scope and enterprise to the work of the now famous Manhattan Engineering District program that culminated in the development of the Atomic Bomb. Just as the latter was primarily an undertaking involving physics and chemistry, so the former will rely largely upon social sciences and philosophy for its basic techniques and assumptions." Invoking the name of the already mythic Manhattan Project, a common tactic for such social science endeavors, was meant to convey to citizens and policy makers not only the thought that such an effort would require the infusion of massive amounts of public money but also the promise that Americans might expect from such an investment a payoff of civilization-saving proportions. The bomb, made possible by the work of the scientific Manhattan Project, had saved the world from fascism; now we needed an equivalent social science Manhattan Project to save us from the bomb and from ourselves.

The Manhattan Security Project barely got beyond the planning stages, and its research plan reveals an unfocused conceptualization of how its mission was to be achieved. Prefaced with the truism that "the attainment of genuine World Peace is today the most urgent need of the human race," the plan goes on to state: "The peace which contemporary man desires is not merely the absence of war. . . . Psychologically it involves the positive manifestations of love and affection in all our essential human relations."[26] A list of the "research issues" on which the project intended to produce "fresh data" included:

Exploration of the effect of emphasis on likenesses versus differences or strengths versus weaknesses between people and nations, in promoting attitudes favorable toward peace or toward war.

Is there any substantial basis for the hope that transnational attitudes can replace nationalism in the modern world?

Relation of the normal development of sex differences and sex relationships to positive social attitudes?

What are the psychological variables or correlates associated with consistent kindness among children and adults?[27]

As vague and generalized as these lines of inquiry are, the plan states that "even before any tested new findings are released, widespread public distribution of existing pertinent knowledge in the this area should be undertaken," because of the "pressing emergency nature of the international situation."[28] How, exactly, fresh data about such issues would address the "pressing emergency nature" of the atomic dilemma was never clearly stated.

Others felt that social-science research should specifically focus on the people who were making the decisions about war and peace. The political scientist Terence Ball has written of the postwar period: "Physicists might say how atoms behaved and engineers how weapons worked, but social scientists could explain, predict—and possibly alter—the behavior of those who pulled the triggers."[29] Similarly, in a 1947 speech titled "Mental Hygiene in a World Crisis," the psychiatrist Jules H. Masserman implored his audience to think that "the men and women of good will in every land must concentrate immediately on the psychological enlightenment of our representatives in power . . . to avert what is probably the final crisis of mankind."[30]

Atomic bombs effected the splitting of atoms (fission) to release energy triggering a fission chain reaction that released immense amounts of energy at once. This model could also be used to suggest how human violence could scale up on a societal level to cause war. "In the beginning, we generally select some weak persons or group as our scapegoat," Masserman cautioned in 1947, but this "system may expand into a sweeping social paranoia, replete with spreading phobias, fantastic witch-hunts, increasingly elaborate ideas and dangers of persecution, and finally, acts of panic-ridden reprisal which lead to the ultimate insanity of war."[31] This was the way interpersonal human violence escalated into warfare. And when nuclear weapons were added to this social dysfunction, civilization itself became the victim.

The problem of the atomic age was conceived as the empowerment of this collective tendency toward violence with the technology of nuclear weaponry. Robert Maynard Hutchins expressed the realist point of view: "Atomic war will be the most horrible we have known, and both the victor and the vanquished will lose it. But, since men have been willing to involve themselves in conflicts in which five million human beings were killed in four years, it seems unlikely that they will abstain in the future merely because forty million human beings may be killed in half an hour."[32]

The solution was a world government, but even this could only be accomplished through the transformation of the human personality. "Civil war may come within the world state if it is organized before there is a world community to support it," Hutchins claimed. The key was to work to raise the consciousness of humans and to establish more effective bonds between them: "Since the great aim is a world community, the great task is education. A world community can exist only with world communication," he urged. "The task is overwhelming, and the chance of success is slight. We must take that chance or die."[33]

The Nobel Prize–winner Bertrand Russell shared both Hutchins's enthusiasm and his skepticism. "To generate the kind of sentiment which (one hopes) will ultimately make world unity a real thing, first leaders and then populations must undergo a long process of re-education. We must learn to think and feel collectively," he wrote. But such an effort was far from guaranteed, because "at present, no one effectively cares for mankind as a whole."[34] Nationalism, loyalty to individual nation-states, was the culprit.

Lewis Mumford disputed the notion that interpersonal violence is the source of social violence and placed that source in society itself, claiming that "efforts to impute the origin of war to some primal animal instinct toward murderous aggression against his own kind are empty rationalizing." War, according to Mumford, came into being because of the psychological dysfunctions of the state, not the individual. He argued that it was the ascent of kings at the dawn of modern civilization in Egypt and Mesopotamia that led to the tradition of warfare. In their attempts to present themselves as gods, kings engaged in an escalating series of actions that culminated in attacks on neighboring societies in order to obtain humans for slavery and sacrifice to bolster their supernatural status. It was not human nature but the will to power that inflicted the tradition of warfare onto humankind.

This analysis fits into Mumford's description of human society as advancing through specific "ages" that are tied to the dominant economies of the time (hunting, agriculture, mercantilism, industry). The transition to an agricultural society, with its fixed cities and increasing populations, effected a profusion of technologies that increased the powers of the social leaders, who felt themselves separate from the common people of their civilization. "Just as the prelude to the nuclear age came with the large-scale introduction of water, wind, and steam power, so the first steps toward civilization were taken in the neolithic domestication of plants and animals." These leaders had a sense of entitlement that, they felt, must be supported by demonstrations of their power and divinity: "Should we be surprised that the achievements of our own age of nuclear power appeared first at the period of myths and fantasies associated with the gods? Absolute power, power to create and annihilate."[35] Mumford continued: "The most formidable threat we confront, perhaps, is the fact that the fantasies that governed the ancient founders of civilization have now become fully realizable. Our most decisive recent inventions, the atom bomb and the planetary rocket, came about through a fusion of the secular and the 'sacred' power . . . the resources of an all-powerful state and the intellectual resources of an all-knowing corps of scientists."

Mumford here hit the mark where many other social scientists fell short. The accepted wisdom, echoed throughout much of the social-science critique, places the blame for the nuclear predicament on the presence of a violent streak innate to human nature. This analysis was both a simplification and an idealization of the problem into one that could be seen as "natural" rather than "structural." It placed the blame collectively on human beings rather than on those who effectively organized society in order to accrue and exercise power. While innate human violence certainly had a role to play in the arms race and the Cold War, it was militarism that was the deeper and more dangerous problem. Militarism is more than the collective violence of a group of human beings; it is the organization of the population and resources of a society in support of aggressive military activities, generally reinforcing the concentration of wealth and power in the hands of those at the helm. "War," Mumford wrote, "was an integral part of the constellation of civilized institutions, held in tension within the city, on the basis of a division of classes, slavery and forced labor, and religious uniformity. To remove any part of this fabric seemed, to the rulers of men, a threat to every other part. They exalted the sacrifices of war because they wanted to maintain their own power."[36]

The atomic age was fraught with peril. The problem was not scientific inquiry, which simply determined the structure of the subatomic world; nor was it the fact that the bomb was added to the human arsenal during a brutal and bloody war. The dilemma that the social scientists sought to cure was what humans would do with this technology now that it had been obtained. The consensus that the danger lay in the innate human capacity for violence missed the more ominous characteristic, which was that humans could be selfish and, when they found themselves in position to do so, could hoard the wealth of a community and imperil its members for personal gain. In an industrial society, this end is often attained through militarism. It was not violence that would take humans to the edge of nuclear oblivion, but greed. "In retrospect," the historian Ellen Schrecker writes, "it is clear that nuclear warfare aside . . . the Cold War actually bolstered the positions of political elites on both sides. Positing a struggle against an implacable, expansionist enemy made it possible to build up a militarized economy and clamp down on dissent."[37]

The Nuclear Shadow: Enabling the Psychological Bomb

Bolstering the position of the elites would prove to be very fruitful. Terence Ball has noted that public support for the social sciences did expand dramatically during the Cold War years. "Measured in almost any terms," Ball writes, "the postwar period proved a bountiful one for the social sciences." He specifically points to the integration of the social sciences into American international expansion as the central thrust of this expansion: "The remarkable growth of the social sciences in postwar America was intimately tied to the growth of American power abroad and of the central government at home."[38] Emblematic of that growth was the employment of large teams of social scientists in the nuclear weapons complex itself.

The effective integration of nuclear weapons into the strategies and tactics of the U.S. military was a primary task during the emerging Cold War, even before the Soviet Union developed nuclear weapons at the end of 1949. Initial military assessments recognized the insufficiencies of existing strategies to fully exploit the potential impact of the new weapons on an adversary. The scale of destruction made possible by the immense yields of the new bombs had fundamentally altered the effectiveness of existing military doctrines. What was needed was a new way of thinking about fighting a war and defeating an enemy.

The strategic merit of the bomb was evaluated in the top-secret "Final Report of the Joint Chiefs of Staff Evaluation Board for Operation Crossroads," dated June 30, 1947.[39] In several places the report called for the establishment of technical boards charged with evaluating the "psychological aspects of atomic warfare," and it specifically called for the inclusion on these boards of "civilian experts in various fields, especially the fields of mass psychology, political history and sociology." The boards were also to focus on the crucial work of the "analysis and classification of targets."[40]

In 1946, the Army Air Corps (soon to become the U.S. Air Force) contracted with the Douglas Aircraft Corporation to create a think tank that would later became the RAND Corporation.[41] At RAND, social-science professionals were integrated into the work of analyzing strategic nuclear issues. Among the most prominent of the nuclear strategists with backgrounds in the social sciences were Bernard Brodie, a political scientist; William Borden, a lawyer; and Albert Wohlstetter, a logician. Both Brodie and Wohlstetter worked at RAND during the 1950s and 1960s.[42]

Brodie, among the first and certainly the best-read of the nuclear strategists, joined the chorus of his colleagues in echoing William Fielding Ogburn when he spoke to a University of Michigan audience in the spring of 1947; on that occasion, he claimed that the chief dilemma confronting modern man was "the dilemma of ever widening disparity in terms of accomplishment and magnitude of consequences between man's physical inventions and his social adaptation to them."[43] But by 1964, when Brodie looked back at his work on nuclear strategy, he could claim that "a majority of those who have made their mark as theorists in [nuclear] strategy have been trained as economists."[44]

Brodie, who was the chief architect of deterrence theory (which holds that the main purpose of nuclear weapons is to act as a deterrent to war), would ironically come full circle in his beliefs. "By the end of his life," the historian Gregg Herken points out, "Brodie had become disillusioned with the subject that he helped to inaugurate as a career. His interests had turned progressively away from nuclear strategy to a topic he evidently considered even more important and tangible—the human and psychological motivations behind war."[45]

Among the first psychologists under contract to the RAND Corporation to study the psychological effects of atomic attacks was Irving L. Janis of Yale. His 1949 study "Psychological Aspects of Vulnerability to Atomic Bomb Attacks" demonstrated that psychological expertise could assist in the planning of an atomic war. Sounding much like his colleagues who were working to transcend nuclear conflict, Janis wrote: "Long before any wartime disaster occurs, there may be a high degree of *psychological* vulnerability to the atomic bomb threat. As the attention of the American public becomes focused more and more upon international tensions and the possibility of another war, the increasing realization that our cities may be destroyed and that millions of American civilians may be killed or mutilated can in itself become a powerful stimulus capable of arousing intense emotional reactions. Any effort on the part of the government to reduce the over-all vulnerability of the US to A-bomb attacks will require careful planning in terms of the psychological factors."[46] In a paradox typical of the Cold War, Janis's article was reprinted in the *Bulletin of the Atomic Scientists*, a primary vehicle of the scientists' movement that was working against any planning for nuclear war.[47]

"In the event of an atomic disaster, even those survivors who are not casualties from emotional shock will be in an extremely aroused state," Janis wrote. "The mere sight of the vast devastation and the hideous sights of the dead and dying will produce a terrifying effect upon almost everyone in the area of disaster. . . . Many persons might also be extremely apprehensive about the possibility that they may have been exposed to lethal amounts of radiation." This was where the psychologist comes in. "How can inappropriate, disorganized, and maladaptive responses be prevented? To some extent the prior training of the general population will be useful in preparing people to act intelligently in a disaster."[48] Concerns such as those expressed by Janis would form the bedrock of much of the efforts of the Federal Civil Defense Administration during the subsequent decades of the Cold War. This effort would see an equal focus on physical and psychological preparations for enduring and recovering from nuclear war.[49]

Planning and preparation was the key: "What can psychiatry and its allied professions, psychology and sociology, contribute to the prevention of untoward mass reactions and to the prevention of individual personality disorders" in the wake of a nuclear attack, asked the psychiatrist Dale C. Cameron, the assistant director of the National Institute of Mental Health in 1950. "To counteract possible unrealistic attitudes of fear and futility, individuals need to be given positive information concerning the effect and particularly the limitations of new weapons." But the simple presentation of facts would not be enough: "Emotional and psychological involvement with facts and plans is as essential as intellectual understanding." The key, according to Cameron, was in training civil defense group leaders who could distribute this information in group settings, where the psychology of group dynamics would reinforce the value of the data: "The 'group' would therefore seem to provide a setting in which necessary information can be given to the individual in a way that will enable him to channelize his anxieties constructively."[50]

But a more immediate and practical application of these theories

7. A medic tags a psychological casualty as unfit for duty after a nuclear explosion in the Army Special Weapons Project 1958 training film *Management of Psychological Casualties.*

beckoned, as there were soon hundreds of thousands of Americans for whom simulated nuclear warfare was becoming a reality. This group consisted of American servicemen participating in nuclear weapons tests in Nevada and in the Pacific.

In addition to helping us learn how to best fight a nuclear war, psychology came to play a key role in preparing U.S. servicemen to fight on the atomic battlefield and to adapt to nuclear weapons (fig. 7). In 1948, Colonel James P. Cooney, the chief of the Radiological Branch, Division of Military Application, of the nascent Atomic Energy Commission (AEC), told an audience of his conclusions after having participated in nuclear weapons testing: "I have observed the reactions of the military, who were not acquainted with the technical details on two missions, Bikini and Eniwetok, and the fear reaction of the uninitiated is appalling." The solution seemed obvious: "Psychological training for the military level of acceptable radiation hazard is possible and should be prosecuted, even if operational training is not."[51]

In 1951, the Pentagon contracted with researchers at two universities to design and analyze programs intended to educate and motivate soldiers in order to better prepare for nuclear war.[52] These programs and materials were to be tested on military personnel scheduled to take part in battlefield maneuvers during upcoming atomic tests. The soldiers would then be tested for their responses to the materials, so that they might be refined and improved. In this way, the atomic soldiers were to become both physical *and* psychological guinea pigs.

The tests were designed to assess the effectiveness on the soldiers of various indoctrination techniques and to gauge their responses to the weapons detonations. The psychological exercises and the briefings they reinforced also functioned to instruct the soldiers in how to feel about the bomb, encouraging them to see it as just another extension of the machinery of warfare.[53]

The two programs set out to measure two different sets of data. Psychologists from George Washington University in Washington, D.C., established the Human Resources Research Office (HumRRO), which focused on gauging the effectiveness of the education and indoctrination programs presented to troops who took part in atomic tests. HumRRO researchers administered questionnaires before and after soldiers participated in tests to determine if they had retained the information they had received during the briefings in Nevada and if the briefings had successfully alleviated their fear of the weapons.[54]

Human-behavior specialists from the Johns Hopkins University Operations Research Office (ORO) set out to measure troops' levels of fear and anxiety during the actual weapons tests.[55] While HumRRO worked to gauge the effectiveness of indoctrination efforts aimed at the servicemen, ORO researchers sought to measure the anxiety and fear among participants in weapons tests through such somatic indicators as heart rate and perspiration rate before, during, and after the tests. ORO's physical measurements detected much higher levels of anxiety than HumRRO's assessments, which were largely based on voluntary responses to written questionnaires.[56]

"A major objective of this exercise," HumRRO's Technical Report No. 1 stated, "was to evaluate psychologically the troops' reactions to the maneuver, before indoctrination, after indoctrination, after the detonation, and after a lapse of about three weeks. Attitude research techniques as well as psychological measures were used to estimate (1) the effectiveness of the indoctrination procedures in increasing the troops' knowledge about atomic warfare and (2) the effects of the detonation, together with its accompanying consequences, on the troops' confidence in their ability to do well in A-bomb fighting."[57]

The HumRRO analysis of Desert Rock IV in 1953 concluded that there was evidence of "both the presence of fear . . . and the absence of disruption of performance." However, the conclusion that the performance was not impaired should not be considered grounds for not funding a further, more nuanced study, since "less easily observed aspects of fear may be important in serving to prepare or energize men to react in an emergency situation."[58]

The results of these studies were integrated into military planning for the atomic battlefield. Writing in the magazine *Army* in 1956, General John E. Dahlquist advised that "the way the survivor of an atomic blast reacts depends on how well his leaders have prepared him for this moment. If they have led him well he will, *at this supreme moment*, become his own leader."[59]

There were, however, voices of dissent within the military. Some of these critics thought that the preparation of soldiers to perform on the atomic battlefield should go beyond indoctrination and exposure to blasts from "safe" distances. In 1959, Major John T. Burke, an Army human-engineering specialist, advocated "shock training." He theorized that unless troops were exposed to the realistic horrors of nuclear war, lectures would be useless. Burke proposed a nuclear shock course, where "within appropriate radii of ground zero, every horror of the nuclear battlefield will be duplicated as realistically as possible. The area will be strewn with blood and plastic replicas of dismembered human bodies. Sickening stenches will emanate from carcasses and chemicals . . . on every side he will be attacked by blinded comrades." Only through such training, he felt, could soldiers truly be expected to perform adequately in actual nuclear combat. "Eventually this procedure will engender both respect for nuclear effects and confidence through familiarity."[60] Burke clearly felt that the performance of soldiers on the atomic battlefield depended more strongly on their ability to deal with shock and horror than it did on their indoctrination, a perspective he termed *realism*.

≡≋≡

This failure of groups like the Manhattan Security Project was a failure of diagnosis. For many of the social scientists called to action by the advent of nuclear weapons, it was a given that the problem was rooted in human nature. Since the beginning of civilization, violence had been a disturbing hallmark of human societies and human behavior. Many of the social-science committees formed to "solve" the nuclear crisis assumed that by focusing on violence, they could isolate and treat the disease of which nuclear weapons were merely technological enablers. This assumption was flawed; the will to amass nuclear weapons and to engage in nuclear war were not simply manifestations of violent human nature but rather were rooted in the long history of militarism, which is more rightly understood as a means to accrue power and wealth. As well-intentioned as their efforts were, by focusing on the potential for violence in individuals and not on the motivating forces behind violence as it is carried out by societies, the social scientists missed the mark.

Lewis Mumford's differentiation between interpersonal human violence and the social activity of war would resonate with social scientists as the Cold War entered the 1960s, an era marked both by the failures of military adventurism and by social protests against militarism. The UCLA psychiatrist Judd Marmor, president of the Academy of Psychoanalysis, wrote in 1963 that "one of the most persistent psychological barriers" to the peaceful resolution of the Cold War was "the widespread assumption that war is an intrinsic manifestation of human nature. This assumption grows out of the theory that war is an inevitable social expression of a fundamental instinct for destructive aggression in man." Marmor cited the naturalist Henry Fairfield Osborne's observation that, in fact, war is quite uncommon in nature. "Modern behavioral scientists," Marmor reported, "in increasing numbers are coming to the conclusion that man's violence is *not* spontaneously instinctive."[61]

The Committee on Social Issues of the Group for the Advancement of Psychiatry, of which Marmor was the chairman, published the booklet *Psychiatric Aspects of the Prevention of Nuclear War* in 1964. Its opening sentence declares, "One of the primary problems that confronts the behavioral scientists in considering the psychological issues involved in the nature of war is the widespread assumption that war is an inexorable consequence of the nature of man and that all efforts to eliminate it are therefore doomed to failure." This statement was based on the belief that "since war requires destructive acts from individual soldiers, it must be the collective expression of individual aggressiveness and hostility."[62]

This committee included a young psychiatrist named Robert J. Lifton, who would go on to do groundbreaking work on the nature of historically based trauma; his seminal study of the psychology of the survivors of Hiroshima and Nagasaki advanced the theory of "psychic numbing," which contributed to subsequent theories of post-traumatic stress disorder.[63] In response to the massacres committed at My Lai by American servicemen in Vietnam, Lifton formulated the theory of atrocity-producing situations. "Atrocities are produced by desperate men—in the case of My Lai, by men victimized by the absolute contradictions of the war they were asked to fight," he wrote in 1971; "The widespread feeling of being stuck in an atrocity contributes, in ways we can now hardly grasp. . . . For nothing is more conducive to collective rage . . . than a sense of being bound to a situation perceived to be both evil and suffocating."[64]

Here we see social-science theories of the roots of warfare coming full circle. No longer seen as centered in the individual inclination to violence, war is depicted as an innately social creation in which the individual is compelled by circumstance to commit abnormal acts of violence. Still, Lifton felt himself to be an isolated voice: "I am struck by how little my own profession has had to say about the matter—about the way in which aberrant *situations* can produce collective disturbance and mass murder."[65]

What is more striking, however, is that even as the social-science profession began to center the source of the violence endemic to war in the state rather than the individual, it had little to say on Lewis Mumford's larger assertion that it is the desire to obtain and protect wealth and power that drives social violence. The pathology of militarism remains to be analyzed.

4

Survival of Self and Nation under Atomic Attack

> There are no civilians, we are all at war.
>
> *Announcement by the U.S. president after a nuclear war in the film* Panic in Year Zero *(1962)*

You Can Survive!

On the night of July 25, 1961, President John Kennedy spoke to the nation about the Berlin crisis, a situation in which the United States and the Soviet Union tiptoed toward nuclear confrontation. "In the event of an attack, the lives of families which are not hit in a nuclear blast and fire can still be saved—if they can be warned to take shelter and if that shelter is available. We owe that kind of insurance to our families—and to our country," he said. Kennedy's linking the destiny of individuals and the family with the national fate gave expression to a primary narrative about the likelihood in early Cold War America of surviving a nuclear explosion. He further informed a stunned nation (about to embark on a fallout-shelter craze in response to his speech) that the government had under development "a new household warning system," the National Emergency Alarm Repeater (NEAR). He spoke of the "sober responsibility" of preparing for nuclear war, and he placed the nation's shelter program under the control of the Department of Defense.[1] These revelations reinforced an awareness that had already dawned on many Americans: they were soldiers in the Cold War, and their backyards were the front line. Their personal survival had become emblematic of the survival of the nation.

Discussions and depictions of survivors following a nuclear war were common in early Cold War America. The Federal Civil Defense Administration (FCDA) and other federal agencies advanced some of these images, but others reached Americans through the mass media and popular culture. At the same time that the U.S. military worried about defeating the Soviet Union in a nuclear war, American citizens worried about surviving one.

Civil defense pamphlets postulated that individuals would survive an atomic attack much as they had always survived natural disasters: good citizenship would lead to survival, and survivors would help society to recover and rebuild. These pamphlets tended to be highly depoliticized: the atomic attacks are of unspecified origin. The pamphlets' depictions of nuclear attack often stressed the metaphoric bond between self and nation, underlining the idea that personal survival equaled national victory.

Like so many other aspects of popular culture in the nuclear age, survival narratives changed markedly in 1954, when the Cold War crossed the threshold into the thermonuclear era. Survival narratives of the latter half of the atmospheric testing era (1954–63) became far more brutal than those of the earlier atmospheric period (1945–54) had been. Narratives of the later period tend to be more fatalistic, portraying aggressive self-interest as a key to survival, even depicting nuclear war as an inevitable event that no one will survive. Public debate mirrored this brutality, as Americans and their clergy debated the ethics of killing neighbors in order to survive a nuclear detonation. This world no longer mirrored the depersonalized community depicted in the civil defense literature of the early atmospheric period; now survival became its own justification.

Popular culture texts tended to emphasize personal character traits as the key to survival, from rugged individualism to violent self-interest and deeply antisocial behaviors. These narratives of survival emphasized the idea that it might be necessary for society to be largely destroyed in order for "our way of life" to continue, thus also linking personal behavior to the behavior of the state. Even though the possibility of nuclear war was terrifying to many Americans, the logic of its necessity and inevitability was personalized and justified in stories of individual survival. The correspondence of self and nation in survival narratives implicitly linked the ethos of personal survival with the necessity of national nuclear conflict.

In popular culture narratives of survival, the individual is removed from society, isolated, while the grotesque surgery of nuclear warfare is performed. These narratives assume that, to make it through this period of intense self-reliance and isolation, it might well become necessary for people to revert to a primitive level of behavior and to commit acts that in peacetime would be considered abhorrent. All such acts were justified by the extremity of the situation and by the imperative to survive, and all must be considered acts of self-defense.

Survival narratives made little reference to the facts about actual survivors in Hiroshima and Nagasaki, where the residents' fate was largely determined by their location relative to ground zero rather than by good citizenship or personal character traits.[2] Since actual survival and the injuries from both the explosion and subsequent radiation damages were facts too horrific and fatalistic to be depicted in texts designed to assure Americans that they could survive an atomic attack, survival narratives instead told powerful stories of personal and national life and death. Ultimately, these fables became tales of impotence in the face of the increasingly destructive power and radioactivity of thermonuclear weapons.

Survival and shelter culture in the early Cold War years is best examined around the three periods of peak activity (outlined in the introduction) that occurred in reaction to larger events. The initial peak period was in the immediate aftermath of the test of the first Soviet atomic bomb (called Joe 1), in late 1949, which led to the first flurry of survival guides in 1950. The next peak was in the period immediately after the successful development of H-bombs in the mid-1950s. The final and most intense peak was the period immediately after the 1961 speech by President Kennedy cited at the beginning of this chapter; this period lasted through the Cuban Missile Crisis of 1962.

Survival Equals Victory

In the 1950s, civil defense publications dedicated to discussing an atomic attack equated survival with victory. In depoliticized pamphlets distributed in the tens of millions, atomic bombs fell as if out of the blue, and the job of the citizen was to survive the explosion. Survival was the endpoint in almost every publication about nuclear war produced by the FCDA. There was never any discussion of war itself, and the social aftermath of an atomic explosion was portrayed merely as a simple matter of cleaning up the debris.

"You Can Survive," proclaimed the opening words of *Survival under Atomic Attack: The Official U.S. Government Booklet*.[3] Twenty million copies of this pamphlet were distributed through the National Security Resources Board in 1950, in the immediate aftermath of Joe 1. This first mass-distributed text on atomic attacks barely mentioned the word *war* and made no mention whatever of the Soviet Union. It described the effects of atomic weapons and told readers what to do to survive atomic explosions, but these events ran their course in a political vacuum; there was little talk of a larger war and none of national victory. "If you follow the pointers in this little booklet you stand far better than an even chance of surviving the bomb's blast, heat, and radioactivity"—it was that simple.[4] *Survival under Atomic Attack* was a training manual on how to prepare for the effects of an atomic explosion because that was the whole point of civil defense: to survive the impact of atomic weapons.

In civil defense pamphlets, the battles of atomic warfare were waged, not against the enemy, but against the effects of the enemy's bombs; if you survived, the United States had survived. "Your own back yard may be tomorrow's front line," the 1951 booklet *This Is Civil Defense* declared. The equivalence of self and nation, the common destiny of the two, is emphasized throughout the narrative. The booklet concludes: "The outcome of modern war is not necessarily decided by armies in the field. Wars today can be won or lost on the home front. The home front cannot be hidden, and it cannot retreat—not if we are to survive as a free people. That puts the problem squarely up to you."[5]

One illustration in the 1953 pamphlet *What about You and Civil Defense?* shows what appears to be a mother distraught over a dead child in a landscape of nuclear devastation. The caption beside the picture speaks of victory: "To win—the enemy must smash our MORALE"; victory was a matter of will. "Either in the foxholes or in our cities," the accompanying text states, "it takes training and guts to stand up under attack—and come back fighting." If you survived, you had succeeded in the difficult business of atomic war. "Can we survive a grand-slam attack on our country?" the pamphlet asked. The answer was emphatic: "Certainly—if we are prepared on the home front. History shows that there is a defense against every weapon ever invented. Modern civil defense is the civilian's program for protecting people, property, and production in case war comes. If the people are prepared, nothing the enemy can hit us with can knock us out."[6]

"If you were a soldier, you would be trained to take care of yourself and keep on fighting," *This Is Civil Defense* reminded its readers. "As a defender of the home front, you must learn to protect yourself and keep on working. . . . One of the chief aims of civil defense is to help you to stay at work no matter what may come. Unless all of us kept at our jobs in the face of attack, the enemy would win the war."[7]

Even though Americans were encouraged to survive so that they could continue to work, civil defense pamphlets usually stressed the concept that they would have to survive nuclear war either alone or in family units. It was up to American individuals, under the guidance of national experts, to win a nuclear war. The 1952 civil defense pamphlet *What You Can Do Now!* was structured as a guide to family survival. It called on Americans to take the "home defense pledge." The first step was to "prepare your home and your family against enemy attack." It listed a ten-step program for family civil defense training (step 6 was to "learn simple steps your family should take to protect yourselves against germ and biological warfare") and included an "air-raid alert card" that was to be posted in the home and carried in wallets. National defense is in your hands, the pamphlet hinted: "an attack . . . may never come if you do your part NOW to make America strong."[8]

When it came to thermonuclear war, the same message of equating survival of the self and family with the survival of the nation prevailed. *Facts about the H-Bomb*, a 1955 civil defense pamphlet aimed at easing fears about the development of thermonuclear weapons, advised Americans to "learn and practice civil defense preparedness in your home, your neighborhood, your community. Then, no matter what happens, you and your family—and the Nation—will be ready." Citizens were called on to "Prepare your home. (1) Get a civil defense disaster first aid kit. (2) Learn how to use it. (3) Practice fire-safe housekeeping. (4) Learn to fight small fires. (5) Maintain a 3-day emergency supply of food and water at all times. (6) Equip the most protected place you can find in or near your home for an air-raid shelter. (7) Know how to practice emergency sanitation measures if necessary. . . . Knowing these things can help save America."[9] President Kennedy emphasized the connection between individual civil defense preparation and national survival in his introduction to the September 1961 issue of *Life* magazine, devoted to fallout shelters. To "protect yourself," he said, was to "strengthen your nation."[10]

In *Civil Defense and Higher Education*, a 1954 booklet prepared by the Committee on Civil Defense and Higher Education of the American Council on Education, citizenship was stressed; individual citizen-survivors voted for continued American civilization with their preparedness: "The techniques of survival, and the concepts of civil defense, are contingent upon the recognition of individual responsibility." The role of institutions of higher learning was "to instill a sense of the duties of citizenship," a mission that "will have a direct bearing on the success of the civil defense program."[11] A civil defense advocacy group called the Civilian Protection Group made the connection explicit in its outline for volunteer leaders: "Civil defense is actually democracy at work."[12]

Self Defense Is National Defense

During the late 1950s, the primary focus of civil defense research and grants shifted to community projects, such as designs for shelters in schools and factories.[13] Yet popular portrayals of survival almost never involved people at work, in school, or in traffic. In official narratives and in the popular imagination, one individual, or one individual's family, was the unit of survival. "Each family was to buy its own wagon train," Tom Engelhardt writes of the family fallout shelter, and he points out that such shelters represent personal resourcefulness in the traditional American grain.[14]

As bombs fall around them, survivors retreat into their home shelters and survive as best they can until civil order is restored. This essential narrative can be found in most civil defense pamphlets for mass distribution and in most of the popular writings of nongovernmental "experts" on survival. Survival was usually depicted as an isolating experience, one in which individuals or families remained in their shelter for days or weeks at a time, emerging only at the command of authorities, who could be counted on to monitor radiation levels and restore order.[15]

In his popular mass-market guide, *How to Survive an Atomic Bomb*, Richard Gerstell anticipated a question readers might well ask when he explained that in preparation for an atomic explosion they should lie down and cover their faces, even for an hour if they had to. "So I may have to lie there for fifteen or twenty minutes or longer on my face in a cellar, and then, if there's actually a raid, I have to lie there all through it. What should I think about, lying there? I'm not kidding. What should I think about?" Gerstell's advice was to recite jingles or, better yet, to try to recall all the advice in his book. This advice was distilled into simple rules for survival: "*Always* shut windows and doors. *Always* seek shelter. *Always* drop flat on your stomach. *Always* follow instructions. *Never* look up. *Never* rush outside after a bombing. *Never* take chances with food or water. *Never* start rumors."[16] In 1950, experts from the Naval Radiological Defense Laboratory in San Francisco grimly advised that "anyone exposed to radiation from an atomic bomb explosion . . . should lie down and keep quiet."[17]

The essentials of survival listed in government civil defense pamphlets of the early 1950s are couched in a familiar how-to format. Structured as guides for the responsible citizen, these texts are matter-of-fact can-do tracts, which supply the tools needed to outwit each of the bomb's effects. If you took the right steps, if you were prepared, if you were vigilant, you could survive the bomb; like insulating your attic, it was a job that, with enough determination and the proper tools, you could do yourself. Preparations for atomic attack even worked their way into federal pamphlets about such disasters as floods and tornadoes. In one pamphlet, *Handbook for Emergencies*, produced by the Defense Department, graphics

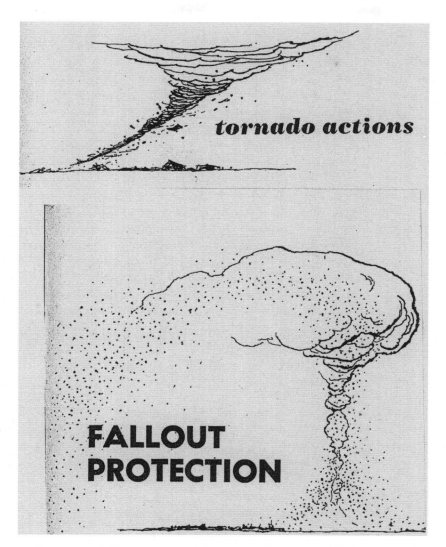

8. Comparing fallout to a natural disaster in the 1963 civil defense pamphlet *Handbook for Emergencies.*

depicting a fallout cloud and a tornado are almost identical (fig. 8).[18] Early popularizers of techniques for surviving the bomb, such as the civil defense consultant Richard Gerstell, frequently utilized this how-to format. A radiation monitor at Bikini in 1946 and a lecturer in radiological defense at the Army Medical Center in Washington, D.C., Gerstell published several articles about survival in 1949 and 1950, in the immediate aftermath of Joe 1, as well as *How to Survive an Atomic Bomb*. Gerstell broke the book into sections variously addressed to apartment or house dwellers and urban or rural populations. "Wherever you live or work, *this book may help save your life*," the inside front cover proclaimed. For each category, Gerstell listed a defense to counteract each bomb effect. He repeated the standard government line that atomic bombs had three effects, blast, heat, and radiation—and that radiation was the only "new effect" of the bomb. "The bomb does give off dangerous atomic rays. . . . They are bad—but not as bad as blast and heat. . . . And there are things you can do to be safe from them—*tested safety steps* for the rays, as well as for the blast and the heat." Every bomb effect had its protective step, and all the steps would add up to survival. Reading the book "will actually make you *feel better*," readers were assured on the back cover. Citing many commonly held fears about atomic bombs, the book promised that "these false ideas, and many others, are nailed down in this fact-filled, easy-to-read book."[19] Government consultants who were selling survival how-to books in a do-it-yourself era made one thing clear: American can-do could solve the problem of survival under atomic attack.

Who Survives?

One essential for life in nuclear-targeted America was a survival kit. Lists of critical materials that citizens should assemble were featured in popular magazines; they were available from the federal government and even from the 4H Council. While a variety of items appeared on these lists, certain essentials—such as an instinctive and potentially violent sense of self-defense—were never mentioned.

Survival, according to government experts, was up to you. If you were prepared and had the guts, you could "make it through." The commodities of survival consisted entirely of materials you could buy ahead of time, ways you should prepare, objects you should gather. These preparations could mean the difference between life and death: "If you know what to expect, what to do, you may come through unharmed even while your neighbors die."[20]

But popular culture clearly expressed the difference between those who survived and those who just had stuff. More basic, and more important than commodities, was another element: being strong enough to survive both the physical destruction of the nation and the collapse of societal boundaries required something special within the individual. In "The Blast," a 1947 story of nuclear war and survival that appeared in *Collier's*, Stuart Cloete sketched a futuristic picture of waiting with his wife in their penthouse apartment following the nuclear devastation of New York City. "We had a second cup of tea. I was surprised how very calm I seemed; my hand hardly trembled. . . . No phone. That, after all, was not surprising after the failure of the electric light. But as the discovery of the telephone had been hailed as a great advance of our civilization, its end—for there was no doubt in my mind that it had ended—was a definite sign that our civilization was disintegrating. We were cut off from the world. . . . We went into the street and found it empty." The protagonist and his wife face postwar New York City utterly alone. Cloete's Last (White) Man ends up using a carbine rifle and riding a horse through Central Park, eventually being taken in by an Indian tribe that had somehow survived and reclaimed Manhattan. A refugee from industrial society, he feels more at home in the irradiated wilderness the park has become.[21]

Television's depictions of surviving an atomic attack also differed from the sanitized portrayal of the civil defense films. The 1950 educational film *You Can Beat the A-Bomb* showed a family surviving a nuclear attack in its basement shelter; it depicted the equivalent of a strong thunderstorm followed by the father's admonition that, after the explosion, it was time for the family to "clean up." The 1953 civil defense film *Target You*, in its turn, repeated the fundamental message that "you will be prepared, you will know what to do instantly to help insure the survival of you, your family, your country."[22] But in the 1956 film *Warning Red*, produced by Norwood Studios in cooperation with the FCDA, we begin to see some movement away from the standard narrative. The script of *Warning Red* is based on standard civil defense tutoring, demonstrating the proper and improper ways to respond to an atomic attack, but the film's backdrops show a post-attack environment that is much more vivid than any that had been seen in previous films. The narrative of *Warning Red* follows a father on his way home to his family when there is a sudden nuclear attack. It ends with the man reunited with his family, who had sheltered safely at a neighbor's house, but the journey takes place against a far more devastated and horrifying backdrop than audiences were accustomed to. The man himself is significantly more disheveled than earlier survivors had been, as are those he encounters on his journey home. All around him, buildings and cars are in flames, and the general area appears devastated and seems likely to be filled with casualties (although none are shown). He meets people who are clearly in shock; one emotionless woman offers him her baby. He tries to help dig a woman and child out from a basement shelter until the "block warden" tells him to leave her there, saying that although she may be uncomfortable, she is safe in the rubble. Another family is seen huddled around a candle and locked in their home. The post-attack world appears bleak; the man's neighborhood does not look as though it will simply recover from the attack as soon as the residents come out and "clean up."[23]

A 1955 episode of the television series *Medic* depicts a devastated post-attack society on the verge of collapse. The focus of the half-hour drama is the life of Dr. Styner, who in this episode is the designated civil defense medical officer, during the first twenty-four hours following a nuclear attack. The attack itself is simply portrayed as a bright flash and a small amount of impact in the shelter where the civil defense team has gathered after an alert is declared. But throughout the episode, the running narrative of a civil defense broadcaster on the radio tells us that there has been a nuclear attack on more than a dozen American cities, followed by an attack with biological weapons using "airborne bacteria," and that the city—presumably New York—in which the drama is set is filled with rioting and hysteria. The announcer calls for the military to quell the rioting and declares that looters will be shot. Later, he claims that the United States has retaliated massively against the enemy.[24] This then is the big war, Herman Kahn's "spasm war."[25]

Although the protagonist, Dr. Styner, is a civil defense official and the episode follows the work of a civil defense medical unit after a war, the world it portrays is horrifying, and no attempt is made to give comfort about the impact and recovery from nuclear attack, a prevalent theme in the civil defense literature. On the way to the clinic from the shelter, the medical team is turned back because of a firestorm so fierce that they can't proceed. They set up a clinic in a school, where Styner is overwhelmed with the wounded survivors of the attack; his unit is "out of everything" and outside the makeshift clinic the casualties are "backed up for a block." The medical system is so overwhelmed that nothing can be done for the large numbers of patients doomed to die from radiation exposure. There is talk that the fallout has spread to "upstate" regions and that the blast area is too contaminated to recover the bodies of the dead. A young girl is brought on a stretcher, moaning from her injuries. Styner determines that the girl will not live and instructs the nurse to take the girl to "isolation," an area separate from the patients who are awaiting transfer to outlying hospitals. The nurse asks Styner why he doesn't give the girl morphine for her pain. He replies that they "haven't got enough for the ones I can save. I can't spare it for the hopeless cases." The nurse protests: "But it's not right! It's not human! She's suffering, she's in agony!" Styner tells her that they are beyond the kind of medicine she learned in nursing school. "You can call it inhumane—all right, it is. But these aren't our terms, they're the terms that were handed to us." These are not the cheerful survivors we are used to from the civil defense literature, whose good citizenship and can-do attitude ensures the reestablishment of the nation.

Emblematic of the show's portrayal of nuclear war as dehumanizing and horrific is the story of a young boy brought into the clinic immediately after the bombing. Styner examines the cuts on the boy's face and asks him what happened. In a clear dig at the civil defense program that emphasized the importance of "Grandma's pantry" as a model of stocking a shelter with food, he says that glass shards from the jars of preserves cut him in his basement shelter. Styner tells him that the cuts are not serious and that in all likelihood he will be fine. The boy pulls a younger boy into the frame and asks "How about my brother? He can't see." He explains that his brother had run up the stairs to see the flash and was blinded by it and that he threw up four or five times after the detonation. Styner asks the nurse to take the younger boy to the isolation section. The older boy asks if he can telephone his mother, who was downtown when the bomb went off. Styner, knowing that the mother is certainly dead, suggests that a call may be possible later. After the boys are led off, the nurse asks Dr. Styner if the little boy is going to remain blind. Styner replies, "That won't bother him for long. With the amount of radiation he's taken, he'll be dead." In the final scene of the show, another medical team finally relieves Dr. Styner and his crew, and as they are leaving, the older boy comes up to Styner to announce that his brother is dead, less than twenty-four hours after his exposure. Styner hugs the crying boy as the credits begin to run.

Tales such as this presented strong counternarratives to the official civil defense depiction of the impact and aftermath of a nuclear attack. Even as the show reinforced the value of civil defense preparedness and the valiant nature of those who worked hard to prepare for a nuclear attack, it framed that preparedness within the grim reality of a collapsing society and an overwhelmed response to the scale of destruction such an attack would bring.

Some popular culture narratives of nuclear war that began to emerge after the Bravo test in March 1954 postulated the absence of any survivors. In these texts, it is always radiation that kills every last person on earth. Mordecai Roshwald's novel *Level 7* is set entirely underground, in a secret government shelter. Slowly the radiation from the nuclear war above ground seeps down to this lowest level—a level that was supposed to be fallout-proof. Roshwald's protagonist is a government clerk whose job it is to push the button of the push-button war. He becomes the Last Man, but only for a moment before he, too, dies.[26]

In his 1957 bestseller *On the Beach*, the Australian novelist Nevil Shute (who himself was dying of cancer at the time), showed the world nuclear war as seen from its deadly margins. The plot focuses on a group of people in Australia who are waiting for the inevitable and deadly fallout from a major nuclear war to reach their continent. The horror of the story is conveyed by the normalcy with which people live out the last days of their lives, patiently awaiting personal, national, and species death. The story opens a year after a "short war" that ended all contact with the outside world, and Shute's characters inhabit a dark suburban Melbourne, physically undamaged yet doomed to radioactive death as the fallout from the war moves ever deeper into the southern hemisphere. We watch their lives crumble as they face certain death from radiation poisoning. A young naval officer and his wife discuss their impending death:

> "That's the way it is. We've just got to take it as it comes. After all, it's what we've always had to face, only we've never faced it, because we're young. Jennifer [their child] might have died first, of the three of us, or I might have died before you. There's not much new about it."
>
> "I suppose not," she said. "I did hope it all might happen on one day."
>
> He took her hand. "It may quite well do so," he said, "But—we'd be lucky." He kissed her. "Let's do the washing up." His eyes fell on the lawn mower. "We can mow the lawn this afternoon."[27]

The normalcy, the domesticity of the scene contains its quiet and powerful horror: a well-trimmed lawn soon to be littered with corpses. Moira Davidson, the novel's heroine, exits in the very last paragraph echoing the self-inflicted death of the larger society; she commits suicide: "Then she put the tablets in her mouth and swallowed them down with a mouthful of brandy, sitting behind the wheel of her big car."[28]

Between 1954 and 1957, the imagined threat of World War III changed from an air assault in which some bombers would get through with smaller nuclear weapons to a thirty-minute push-button war, in which thousands of missiles would carry hydrogen bombs around the globe in a matter of minutes.[29] Thermonuclear weapons changed the war that

Americans were expected to survive and with it changed the image of the survivor. The conscientious citizen-survivor of the early atmospheric testing era gave way to the rugged survivalist of the H-bomb era.

The film *Panic in Year Zero* was released in 1962, a time when the moral issues implicit in the very idea of fallout shelters had become familiar to the American public. Harry Baldwin, an average American father, is taking his family into the mountains outside of Los Angeles for a little camping and fishing when the big war breaks out. From a gas station outside of town, the family sees the flash of an H-bomb over Los Angeles. We see Harry visibly change; he has only one thought now: survival. After his wife's vain attempts to reach her mother, who is still in Los Angeles, by phone, Harry decides that they will not go back for Mother—they will go into the mountains to survive. It's "'A' day," claimed one of the promotional posters for the movie, "when civilization came to an end."

Now Harry, played by Academy Award winner Ray Milland (who also directed the film), turns cold and calculating. There is no blast damage where they are, and he figures that, since it is early morning, many people might not yet have learned of the attacks, and so they might still sell him supplies, not realizing how valuable these goods have become. Harry's plan works—in a small town he wakes up the owner of a grocery store and buys hundreds of dollars' worth of supplies. He moves on to the hardware store, and when the owner won't take a check for half the goods, Harry pulls out one of the guns he has just bought and ties his fellow citizen up. Harry's son (played by Frankie Avalon as the best-groomed nuclear war survivor ever) joins him in the crime, and accompanied by the horrified looks of the women in their family, they ride off into the mountains.

American society appears to have completely crumbled. In the mountains, Harry sets up a military-style home base, establishing caches of food and weapons outside the family's cave. Both Baldwin children are attacked by a gang of delinquent youths, and when the son is wounded the family is forced to leave the cave shelter in search of medical assistance. After fighting their way through endless vigilante neighbors, the Baldwins find society reestablished, symbolized by the arrival of the Army. Harry again visibly changes; order is restored, his rational side reemerges: all will be well. "You're the Army!" Harry exclaims, smiling. His wife bursts into tears: "Harry, thank God!"[30] The brutal survival skills he called on in defense of his family can recede now, as they have served their purpose: bridging his family's survival from the collapse of society to its restoration.[31]

In *Panic in Year Zero* we see survival at its most socially primitive, as an exercise in personal or familial militarism: those outside the unit of survival were by definition enemies. In this world, all supplies were to be hoarded and hidden; the idea of community was nonexistent. The primitivism shown by Harry, out of place in normal society, expressed the power by which he was able to survive and secure his family's survival.

We have seen how, in civil defense literature, survival became itself a definition of victory in nuclear war. This film takes such logic a step further by showing us a world in which survival is the ultimate morality. Harry Baldwin judges his own actions and those of others only by whether they help his family to survive. Reversion to a primitive state free of social morality is item number one in Harry's survival kit.

Neighbors as Enemies

Speaking in Las Vegas in the spring of 1961, the local civil defense leader J. Carlton Adair called for the creation of a five-thousand-man militia to repel the Californians who would pour in "like a swarm of locusts" after a nuclear attack. Back in California, the same sentiment prevailed: Keith Dwyer, the civil defense coordinator for Riverside County, warned officials in the Riverside County city of Beaumont, a hundred miles west of Los Angeles, to expect 150,000 Angelinos to stream into their town, and he advised all local residents to include a pistol in their survival kits.[32]

The dilemmas posed by the locked doors of fallout shelters were very real: if survival depended on careful planning and preparation, opening a shelter to more people than it was designed to hold might well reduce the odds of survival for everyone. But there were deeper questions, such as how far someone should go in destroying social norms in order to preserve society itself. In justifying self-defense at almost any cost, the various narratives of conflict with neighbors over fallout shelters can be seen as arising out of the dynamics of the larger conflict of nuclear war itself.

These events prompted an April 1961 article in *Time* on Americans who armed themselves in shelters. This article, and the subsequent cultural debate it sparked, even made it as far as *The Twilight Zone*, although, as Margot Henriksen has pointed out, the debate was largely subsumed in the general shelter hysteria that followed Kennedy's speech.[33] Printed in the "Religion" section, the *Time* article was titled "Gun Thy Neighbor?" and sported a picture of one Charles Davis and his family in their Austin, Texas, shelter, armed as though to take down giant irradiated ants. Pointing to a four-inch-thick door, Davis warned, "This isn't to keep radiation out, it's to keep people out." The article opens with the even more startling claim, by an unnamed Chicago suburbanite: "When I get my shelter finished, I'm going to mount a machine gun at the hatch to keep the neighbors out." It also told of a man in Hartford, Connecticut, who informed his neighbor that he would have to shoot her and her baby if she persisted in trying to get into his shelter after an attack.[34]

The *Time* article included comments by six religious authorities, only one of whom, Father Francis Filas, S.J., chairman of the department of theology at Loyola University in Chicago, sanctioned violence as a last resort to keep intruders out of a shelter. "Without any hesitation, I believe one could justify restricting capacity of a fallout shelter because of limited supplies of air, room and the like. But the method of restriction would have to be moral—namely barring the entrance, and not the use of violent means unless intrusion itself was threatened."[35]

After the *Time* article, Father Filas was outgunned by another Jesuit, Father L. C. McHugh, who advised readers, from his post as associate editor for science at the Jesuit magazine *America: A Catholic Review of the Week*, that Christian ethics dictated that one ought to conceal the entrance to a family shelter and place "protective devices" (meaning guns) in the shelter to defend its occupants and contents from "panicky aggressors."[36]

In a September 30, 1961, article in *America* titled "Ethics at the Shelter Doorway," McHugh, provoked by one of the respondents to *Time*'s religious queries the previous spring, set forth his interpretation of the Christian ethics involved in shelter self-defense. McHugh, formerly an ethics professor at Georgetown University, took issue with the Reverend Hugh Saussy of Holy Innocents Episcopal Church in Atlanta, who had responded in the original *Time* article that "if someone wanted to use the shelter, then you yourself should get out and let him use it . . . that's the strict Christian application."[37] McHugh's advice to anyone who agreed with this belief was to "go next door and build [a shelter] for your neighbor. In an emergency, he can take refuge there more quickly if it is on his own property instead of yours."[38]

McHugh proclaimed that Americans "need a little instruction in the grim guidelines of essential morality at the shelter hatchway." Putting the family shelter itself in perspective, he explained that it "is more than a piece of property that should be secure against trespass. It is a property of the most vital kind. When the bombs start falling, it is likely to be the one material good in your family's environment which is equivalent to life itself." Citing traditional Catholic ethical doctrines, McHugh argued that "bonds of both love and justice" made every man responsible for the safety of his wife and children, and that to "squander their essential welfare" was an act of cowardice, not charity. He advised that "if others steal your family shelter space before you get there, you may also use whatever means will recover your sanctuary intact."[39] This suggestion presumably included such steps as those mentioned by Charles Davis in the *Time* article: "I've got a .38 tear-gas gun, and if I fire six or seven tear-gas bullets into the shelter, they'll either come out or the tear-gas will get them."[40]

In his article, McHugh never explicitly stated that people should take "protective devices" into the family shelter; he merely advised that there was no ethical impediment to doing so. But in a subsequent television interview he went much further:

> Let's say you got your family in your shelter, the attack is on, a question might come up of admitting anyone over and above the number for whom the shelter is designed. I'd say that we should rely on the best prudential judgment that the father or the one responsible for the shelter can make in the circumstances. But I say let him think twice before he admits the needy stranger if admitting the needy stranger is going to cut down the chances of survival of the group that's already there. And then that final point: Can a man have protective devices in order to protect his family once they are in the shelter from, let's say, strangers that try to use a crowbar to get in? I'd say, from what I have been talking about, the matter of self-defense, it would be wise for a man to at least weigh the possibility of putting some protective devices in his shelter along with other elements of his survival kit.[41]

This new morality of survival, in which Americans were encouraged to defend a twelve-by-eight-foot hole in the ground and a few dozen cans of food, was based on the premise that even your neighbors might be the enemy in a nuclear war and that survival justifies all acts of self-defense.

Opposition to McHugh's statements abounded in the Christian press. The Episcopal bishop of Washington, D.C., Angus Dun, called his remarks "utterly immoral: the kind of man who will be most desperately needed in a post-attack world is least likely to dig himself a private mole-hole that has no room for his neighbor." Citing the inability of poorer families to afford shelters, Dun noted that "justice, mercy and brotherly love do not cease to operate, even in the final apocalypse."[42] The editors of *Commonweal* took the middle ground, declaring that "if we do not address ourselves to the problems raised by Bishop Dun, we may one day be forced to address ourselves to the problems raised by Father McHugh."[43]

Kenneth Rose argues that the "shelter morality" debate "badly damaged the reputation of the home shelter," and President Kennedy himself joined the debate by saying, "Let us concentrate more on keeping enemy bombers and missiles away from our shores, and concentrate less on keeping neighbors away from our shelters."[44]

Rod Serling, the creator of *The Twilight Zone*, took on the moral dilemmas posed by shelters in an episode televised in the 1961–62 season. Margot Henriksen describes the episode, titled "The Shelter," as having "exposed the loss of human compassion embodied in shelter ethics."[45] Dinner guests who are gathered to celebrate the birthday of a doctor in their community scatter after a radio announcement of an impending nuclear attack. One by one, each appears back at the house of the doctor, the only one among them who has built a shelter. He refuses entry to all of them and locks his wife and himself into the shelter. When the desperate group tries to unite in order to break down the door, each member betrays a hidden hatred of the others. Then the radio announces that what had appeared to be Russian bombers turned out to be geese. The doctor's house, ripped apart by his neighbors as they tried to enter the shelter, is completely destroyed, as is any sense of community on this stretch of suburbia somewhere in the twilight zone. The neighbors offer to pay the doctor for the damage they have done to his house, but he is not so easily appeased: "Damages? I wonder. I wonder if any one of us knows what those damages really are. Maybe one of them is finding out what we're really like when we're normal. The kind of people we are just underneath the skin. I mean all of us. A lot of naked wild animals who put such a price on staying alive that they'll claw their neighbors to death just for the privilege. We were spared a bomb tonight, but I wonder if we weren't destroyed even without it."[46]

If personal survival was to be everyone's sole moral determinant, and self-defense could justify acts that at other times would be seen as abhorrent, we could as easily justify the act of nuclear warfare itself, in which survival was considered victory and the institutions of society could be destroyed in order to preserve the society itself. With the individual and the family removed from society and placed into a primitive world in which survival defines its own morality, the logic of nuclear war survival was in place, but so too was the logic of nuclear warfare.

Ignoring Hiroshima and Nagasaki

The model of survival Americans could look to in anticipation of their own imagined fate was made vivid by media reports of atomic-bomb survivors in Hiroshima and Nagasaki. In the decade following the end of World War II, residents of the two destroyed cities, redeemed by their victimhood from their status as enemy, came to be seen in a different light than that cast on the Japanese in general. In 1946, Americans' mental view traveled downward from the (mushroom) clouds to focus on what had happened on the ground below. The bombing of Hiroshima and Nagasaki had incinerated each city in a split second and had killed almost 150,000 people instantly, with many tens of thousands more to die in the following month or two. But the bombs had also left over 100,000 injured, many of whom did survive.

Survivors of the atomic bombing of Japan were first made real to the American people in the writing of John Hersey. His best-selling book *Hiroshima*, first published in its entirety in the August 31, 1946, issue of the *New Yorker*, was an account of the bombing told from the perspective of a number of residents who survived the attack.[47] Hersey painted a horrifying picture of atomic explosion and survival, as the victims' world collapsed on top of them, one after another. Typical is the story of Toshiko Sasaki, a clerk at the East Asia Tin Works:

> Miss Sasaki went back to her office and sat down at her desk. She was quite far from the windows, which were off to her left, and behind her were a couple of tall bookcases containing all the books of the factory library, which the personnel department had organized. She settled herself at her desk, put some things in a drawer, and shifted some papers. She thought that before she would begin to make entries on her list of new employees, discharges, and departures for the Army, she would chat for a moment with the girl at her right. Just as she turned her head away from the windows, the room was filled with a blinding light. She was paralyzed with fear, fixed still in her chair for a long moment (the plant was 1,600 yards from the center).
>
> Everything fell, and Miss Sasaki lost consciousness. The ceiling dropped suddenly and the wooden floor above collapsed in splinters and the people up there came down and the roof above them gave way; but principally and first of all the bookcases right behind her swooped forward and the contents threw her down, with her left leg horribly twisted and breaking underneath her. There, in the tin factory, in the first moment of the atomic age, a human being was crushed by books.[48]

In Hersey's book, survival is a living hell. The varied tales are united by a common thread of horror: survivors trying to pull charred neighbors from the river (where many sought relief from their severe burns), only to have the flesh come off the victims' hands like gloves; featureless near-dead people piled up and moaning in gutters along the streets. The book ends with children searching for their mothers.

In this narrative, individuality is erased as a critical factor for survivors. "He went to the river again, the basin in his hand, and jumped down onto a sandspit. There he saw hundreds of people so badly wounded that they could not get up to go further from the burning city. When they saw a man erect and unhurt, the chant began again, 'Mizu, mizu, mizu'" (*mizu* is Japanese for water).[49] The dead are depicted as featureless, a mass of dying humanity. The survivors cited the specifics of their location and of the structures in which they found themselves as the key factors of their survival; none spoke of character traits as a contributing factor. While the early months after the bombing of Hiroshima and Nagasaki were filled with concerns about the destructive power of the atomic bomb and speculation about future wars, *Hiroshima* was the first public portrayal of the people who had actually survived an atomic attack. Hersey's book was reprinted widely and serialized on many radio stations.

In 1946, shortly after the publication of *Hiroshima*, the National Committee on Atomic Information released a film in theaters across America that featured footage taken by Allied filmmakers in Hiroshima and Nagasaki after the blast. *One World or None* was one of the first opportunities Americans had to actually see images of the human victims of the bombings, since most print sources showed only images of scorched landscapes devoid of human victims or survivors, images that Spencer Weart has called "dangerously incomplete."[50] The footage in *One World or None* exposed to view scorched human bodies as well as shadows from vaporized bodies flashed like photographs onto streets and walls. It also showed the impersonal images of survivors as they were displayed by the medical personnel who were studying them, their scarred and burned bodies viewed from one angle and then another. These were hardly the rugged individualists that Americans would later encounter in survival literature and in the narratives of popular culture.

At the same time that Americans were being exposed to the realities of Hiroshima and Nagasaki, alarming pictures of future atomic wars were being painted by politically active scientists who were working to promote legislation that would take atomic energy, for good and ill, into account. Joined in what was known as the scientists' movement, these organizations worked to pass the McMahon Bill (1946)—sponsored by Brien McMahon, a Democratic senator from Connecticut—which created the Atomic Energy Commission and established civilian control over the federal government's atomic policy. A second objective of the scientists' movement was to issue broad public warnings about the nature of atomic explosions.

Speakers from activist scientists' groups described nuclear war in a wide variety of forums, from radio programs to meetings of business groups. A program pitched to the Emergency Committee of Atomic Scientists by the public-relations firm Wallace Thorsen Organization stressed that "the message to be 'sold' should not be simply education about the atomic bomb and atomic energy, but about the structure of peace itself and the folly of allowing nationalism to rule men's future. Atomic energy and the bomb should of course be the dramatic 'hook' in this campaign." It was hoped that the focus on the politics of the atomic age would make sure the issue did not "'peter out' once the fear motive has been dulled by exposure."[51]

This narrative of nuclear warfare was the first one widely articulated in American popular culture. The early images of atomic explosions and survival were generally very impersonal, stressing the impact of the weapons on the community rather than on individuals. The narratives typically portrayed the effect of an atomic detonation on the city in which the presentation was being given. The presenters were very cognizant of the model that Hiroshima and Nagasaki had created in the minds of their audiences.

Speaking on the radio in 1946, Dr. Willard Stout of the Association of Los Alamos Scientists told his audience, "It is quite possible that an atomic attack could be launched upon a country such as the United States some morning, and by nightfall forty or fifty major cities would be knocked out, as Hiroshima was knocked out, several tens of millions of people would be dead, our government would be largely incapacitated, our communication system in chaos and those of our people who remained alive in a state of panic."[52]

In *Reader's Digest* in May 1946, Robert Littell asked Major General Thomas F. Farrell, the second-in-command of the Manhattan Project, what would happen if an atomic bomb were dropped directly on top of the Empire State Building, "If fused correctly, one of those bombs could blow the Empire State Building to hell. There might be some sort of stump left for a few floors above the ground."[53]

The activist groups produced a wide variety of films on atomic explosions as well. The American Federation of Scientists offered frequent showings of footage from Hiroshima and Nagasaki, for example, offering

9. A nuclear explosion results in a skull over Manhattan in the 1946 film *One World or None*.

free showings of the film *A Tale of Two Cities* (made by the Army Signal Corps) at a downtown Baltimore theater on four successive Tuesday afternoons in 1948. In the film *One World or None*, the news commentator Raymond Gram Swing painted this stark picture of a nuclear explosion over New York City:

> Practically everyone within a radius of two miles is killed or injured. Horrible effects of radiation are permanent blindness, sterility, loss of teeth, prolonged bleeding, and ulcerations of the body tissues.
>
> The heat generated is so great that literally nothing remains but dust and smoke. No streets, no walls, not even dead bodies, everything has been pulverized. Fires of terrific dimensions sweep the city.
>
> This is what one atomic bomb does. What would a few dozen atomic bombs do? The answer is quite simple: wipe out practically the whole of New York City and its inhabitants.[54]

One World or None offered a picture of a devastated landscape. Its vision was not of personal death but of a collective demise. The back of the printed pamphlet that accompanied the showings of *One World or None*, titled *This Could Happen in Your City*, showed a skull hovering over Manhattan (fig. 9). Contrasted with the front-cover photo of a vaporized Hiroshima, the message was clear: every town could become a Hiroshima or a Nagasaki.

Americans were again confronted with actual survivors in 1955, when Norman Cousins brought twenty-five Japanese women who had been crippled or disfigured by the atomic bombing of Hiroshima to the United States for reconstructive surgery. These women, who had all been schoolgirls at the time they were injured by the bomb, were called the Hiroshima Maidens in the American press. On May 11 two of them were introduced to America on live TV on the NBC show *This Is Your Life*, hosted by Ralph Edwards. The subject of the episode was a Japanese minister, Reverend Kiyoshi Tanimoto of Hiroshima. The show's format consisted of confronting a weekly subject with people from his or her past; this episode included the bombardier of the *Enola Gay* (the plane that carried and dropped the Hiroshima bomb), a visibly intoxicated Captain Robert Lewis, who cried and told the audience that he wrote "My God, what have we done?" in his log immediately after the bombing.[55] The two victims, Tadaka Emori and Toyoko Minowa, were shown in silhouette only because, Edwards explained, "both are badly disfigured." The women said, in Japanese, that they were happy and grateful to be in America. Seen as pleasant and polite or as wounded victims, they hardly presented the image of the prepared and gutsy survivors who would inhabit the core of the iconology of American survival narratives.[56]

Why was there such a wide gap in American popular culture from 1945 to 1963 between the images of real survivors of atomic weapons and the images of survivors of an anticipated atomic attack? The answer is that narratives of survival were not about the actual survival of individual Americans; they were metaphors for the survival of America itself. Popular images of tenacious cowboy survivors helped Americans to see their personal and the national survival of an atomic attack as heroic, stemming from traditional iconic sources of American strength.

In the atmospheric testing era, the iconography of survival expressed ideals of personal heroism, national survival, individual savagery, and ultimately, human impotence; it had little to do with the actual human survival of a nuclear war. Americans used survival narratives to convince themselves that the world as they knew it ultimately endures. But if survival equaled victory in civil defense narratives, then victory could be defined in a way that allowed for the general destruction of American society and tens of millions of its people, as well as violence against neighbors. Larger issues, such as the questions of what the war was fought over and whether the conflict was worth the loss, never clouded the victory achieved through individual survival.

As the technological development of nuclear weapons transformed the worst fears of nuclear pessimists into actual possibilities, Americans found that it was indeed true that their own survival was linked to that of the larger nation. Faced with arsenals of H-bombs numbering in the thousands, and then tens of thousands, deliverable worldwide with half an hour, the realization of Target America was inevitable. The second half of the Cold War years saw the abandonment of any serious discussion in the United States of public shelters.

American citizens and the U.S. government both survived the Cold War, but the association of self with nation did not. By the end of the Cold War, many Americans had come to look upon their own nation's weapons as just as menacing as the weapons of their enemies. Images of massive global thermonuclear war and of nuclear winter lumped all life on earth into the common group of victims of nuclear war, a group that knew no national borders.

Rod Serling summed up the tensions over survival in the thermonuclear age in his remarks at the end of the *Twilight Zone* episode "The Shelter": "For civilization to survive, the human race has to remain civilized."

5

Good Bomb / Bad Bomb

> Thus we do develop weapons, not to wage war, but to prevent war.
>
> *President Dwight D. Eisenhower, October 23, 1956*

The Good Bomb

In the fall of 1953, *Reader's Digest* brought the voice of Mrs. L. F. van Hagan to a nation adjusting to the regular testing of atomic weapons in the continental United States:

> My son and his family, who live in California not too far from the atomic-bomb testing grounds in Nevada, are becoming used to seeing a flash and some minutes later feeling their house rock. One night recently he woke from a sound sleep and asked, "What's that?"
> "Oh, go back to sleep," said his wife. "It's only an atomic bomb."[1]

This comfort level—"it's only an atomic bomb"—was a feeling that the Atomic Energy Commission (AEC) encouraged among those who lived near the Nevada Test Site (NTS).[2] The dark visions that typified narratives of an atomic attack in popular culture stood in stark contrast to images promoted by the federal government to certain groups of American citizens in whose daily world atomic weapons were a very real presence—the so-called atomic soldiers and the downwinders.

Atomic soldiers refers to military personnel who were engaged in nuclear weapons testing, both in Nevada and in the Pacific. Between 1946 and 1963, 300,000 to 400,000 servicemen, drawn from all branches of the military, took part in one or more atmospheric nuclear test. In 1951 the Army established Camp Mercury alongside the NTS to facilitate the participation of these troops in regular atomic tests in Nevada. At first kept to a distance of seven miles from ground zero, eventually military personnel would experience the blasts from less than four miles away.[3]

Downwinders were those residents of Nevada and Utah who lived in the immediate path of fallout from the tests at the NTS.[4] Diane Nielson, a nurse in Henderson, Nevada, remembered the tests from her childhood: "After a bomb, there it would be, the fallout, fine like flour, kind of grayish white. We would play like that was our snow. We never had snow there because it was a warm climate. Then we would go out and write our names in it. It would be thick enough you could write your name in it and see it. It would burn your fingers, it would irritate you, and you would have to wash your hands."[5] Numbering barely more than a hundred thousand, most of the downwinders were Mormon ranchers and shopkeepers.

These two groups were separately presented with a wide variety of images and texts whose iconography depicted members of their communities feeling at ease in the vicinity of atomic bombs. Both groups were reassured that the bombs going off around them would not hurt them. They were encouraged to see the atomic bomb, and the attendant radiation, as a natural part of their daily lives rather than as a threat. The bomb presented to these specific communities was a beautiful bomb, a Disney bomb.

The AEC believed that a continental testing site was vital to national security. Compared with the Pacific Proving Ground in the Marshall Islands, Nevada had several advantages. Most important, it was cheaper to test weapons in Nevada, since it did not involve the transport and long-term use of naval vessels and their crews. Second, the Nevada site was located just hours away from the two major weapon labs, at Los Alamos in New Mexico and at Livermore in northern California, shortening the time scientists needed to be away from these labs, thus making it easier for them to observe tests. Third, it was significantly simpler to make detailed observations of blasts in the desert than it was of detonations in the ocean.[6] Public fear of radiation and opposition to continental tests were seen by AEC commissioners as the only element that might jeopardize continued use of the NTS.

In an effort to protect the Nevada site from public criticism, the AEC created the counternarrative of a benign atomic bomb, one that gave off a weaker form of radioactivity. In the short term, the AEC managed to reassure both the atomic soldiers and the downwinders and maintain the place of the NTS in the American testing program, but by the late 1950s the AEC had damaged its own credibility on the question of radioactive fallout.

Sharing the Horizon with the Atomic Bomb

From the beginning of nuclear testing in Nevada, the AEC took a very determined approach to public relations with Las Vegas and the downwind communities, and it devised several ways to help the locals feel more comfortable with nuclear explosions. Thermonuclear bombs (fusion or H-bombs) were not tested at this site, only smaller, fission weapons.[7] Clear and trivial claims of property damage—such as the plate-glass

10. A downwind couple shield their eyes from the flash with sunglasses as they enjoy a nuclear explosion in the 1955 AEC pamphlet *Atomic Tests in Nevada*.

windows blown out at two car dealerships in Las Vegas following the first test on February 6, 1951—were quickly paid.[8] AEC employees carried cans of gas to aid motorists stranded in the desert, "compliments of the AEC," as they told the drivers.[9] Speakers were sent into downwind communities to assure residents of their safety, and specially produced educational materials, aimed at easing fears about radiation and bombs, were distributed in these communities. Of particular importance in propaganda terms was the booklet *Atomic Tests in Nevada*, popularly known as the Green Book (see chapter 1), distributed by the AEC to the downwinders first in 1955 and again, in a revised edition, in 1957. The Green Book was a virtual primer on the good bomb written for its good neighbors.[10]

Two graphics from the Green Book show downwinders sharing the horizon with the blast of a nuclear weapon. In the first, a cowboy and his girl demonstrate the proper use of sunglasses as a cloud looms behind them (fig. 10), while the second shows members of the downwind community (cowboy in front) gathered to observe the blast depicted behind them. They are a calm, representative bunch of townsfolk without a worried face among them (fig. 11).[11]

11. The whole downwinder community seems comfortable with a nuclear explosion in *Atomic Tests in Nevada* of 1955.

Downwinders and atomic soldiers were frequently depicted in graphic images that showed them sharing the desert horizon with atomic bombs. None of the people in these images ever showed any fear of the bomb; they were always calm and in control. The accompanying text typically addresses fears about the strength of atomic weapons. The Green Book tells downwinders some good news contained in a summary of fallout studies over the first six years of operation for the NTS, all designed "to pinpoint the degree of possible hazard or inconvenience created by the Nevada tests": that *"simply stated,* all such findings have confirmed that the Nevada test fallout has not caused illness or injured the health of anyone living near the test site."[12]

"You people who live near the Nevada Test Site are in a very real sense participants in the Nation's atomic test program," the Green Book ominously claimed on its second page.[13] These bombs seemed much less threatening than the ones responsible for creating the concentric circles of destruction shown over maps of America's cities in hometown daily newspapers everywhere. Here is the description of an atomic explosion from the Green Book: "The effects of the flash of light are essentially no different from those of sunlight. . . . Shock waves go out in all directions from the detonation. Some strike the earth and are dissipated. Some are reflected back to earth from various atmospheric layers. If they reach earth at an inhabited point, they may be felt or heard."[14] Compare that text with this image of an atomic explosion taken from the nationally distributed 1950 civil defense booklet called *Atomic Attack—A Manual for Survival*:

> A flash. So bright that everyone will swear it comes from whatever direction he happened to be looking.
>
> Then, an instant later, a sudden hammer blow from the air, the stillness broken by a rush of hot wind. Walls of buildings that face the bomb burst, subject to overwhelming pressure, drop off. It will be as though a motorist were blinded by the reflection of the sun from another car's windshield. Except that the light will remain. The man outdoors will have to act on the instant, or be caught standing when the hammer blow hits and the buildings start to fall.[15]

By comparison, the Nevada bombs didn't sound so bad at all.

Even radiation sounded benign in the AEC booklet *Assuring Public Safety in Continental Weapons Tests*, issued in January 1953: "The body may safely receive a small dose of radiation because the effects are repaired virtually as rapidly as they are produced. A large number of small doses may be given over a period of time, as the body is able to repair itself between doses. Over a period of many years, a human being may safely receive a total amount of radiation which would cause a fatal illness if administered to his whole body within a period of a few minutes." Downwinders were repeatedly told that they received far less radiation than was allowed test-site workers.[16]

"We cannot see, feel, taste, or hear nuclear radiation. Consequently it may seem to be more difficult to understand than are light and sound waves from Nevada tests," the Green Book advised. Readers were comforted to learn that fallout from the local tests remained literally over their heads: "For a Nevada shot the air mass containing fission particles remains within the troposphere, which is the atmospheric layer extending from the earth's surface up to about 6 miles. Some particles may take two or three trips around the earth in a given latitude before being entirely removed by the action of precipitation, gravity and atmospheric turbulence, with rain and snow the most important factors." Emphasizing the "protection of the public," the booklet assured readers that "no one outside the test site has been hurt in six years of testing."[17]

Articles published in the magazines and journals of the various service branches featured soldiers calmly sharing the horizon with atomic

12. A marine casually strolls to his foxhole while timing the impact of an atomic blast in an illustration from *Leatherneck: The Magazine of the Marines*, 1953.

explosions. These articles were designed to encourage servicemen to feel unthreatened by atomic weapons. "One of the main things you learn at Exercise Desert Rock," one such article confided, "is that the foxhole is still in vogue. Field fortifications that will afford good protection against conventional bombs and shells will afford good protection against A-bomb blast, heat, and radiation."[18] A 1953 article in *Leatherneck* was accompanied by a drawing that also suggested the foxhole's ability to neutralize the force of an atomic bomb (fig. 12). The article advised that "flash is the key to longer life. At one mile from ground zero you have better than three seconds to get into a hole and set up housekeeping." The drawing shows the Marine's ability to relax and feel at home with a mushroom cloud just up the hilltop. The Marine in the cartoon is casually watering his flower garden and glancing at his stopwatch, caught at two seconds, showing that he has a full second to get down into his personally decorated foxhole.[19] This Marine felt safe in his foxhole only one mile from the detonation—a distance at which real foxholes often collapsed on crouching servicemen.[20]

An image from *Army Combat Forces Journal* from 1955 shows the "survivor," standing tall and defiant, face to face with an enemy atomic blast. He has survived, and can continue fighting, the article assures us. The soldier—a cartoon figure standing in a photograph of a Nevada mushroom cloud—is wearing a ripped shirt but is still determined to win.[21] This same vision of the brave soldier-survivor made it into the February 1956 issue of *Army*, in which General John E. Dahlquist ponders the survivor's reaction to a nuclear attack: "Will he stagger to his feet, thanking the Lord he is alive, and remove himself from the war? Or will he praise God that he has been spared to fight again and begin doing it? Will his soldier's instincts tell him that the enemy's weapon indicates a critical area, a probable attack target?"[22]

Servicemen sent to Camp Mercury were given the "facts" about atomic bombs, and this lesson represented the essence of their atomic indoctrination. The first fact was that the bomb had three effects: blast, heat, and radiation. The second fact was that, simply because radiation was a "new" effect, soldiers were unjustly afraid of it. As the Marines who read *Leatherneck* in 1953 were advised, "Radiation is the only new effect from the A-bomb and it's the least important of the three effects as far as you, the ground troopers, are concerned." Behind all of these military publications was the belief that getting the "facts" about bombs, or about fallout, would automatically change the serviceman's perspective from one of fear to one of comfort.[23]

This attitude can be seen in the September 19, 1952, issue of *Armed Forces Talk*, an inter-service journal for military leadership. The entire issue was devoted to the story "You Go to Desert Rock." According to the opening paragraph, "If you were not among the 7,000 soldiers, sailors, marines, and airmen who received orders to take part in A-bomb tests near Camp Desert Rock, Nevada, in fiscal year 1952, you may be among the greater number scheduled to participate in future tests." Those destined to maneuver beneath the giant mushrooms were told what to expect there: "You will come back deeply impressed by the awesome power that stunned and dwarfed you. But you, and all those to whom you pass the word, will feel a sense of relief at knowing the score. An A-bomb blast does not necessarily signal the end of the game." In fact, "if uninjured by blast or burns, don't worry about flash radiation . . . the decontamination process is relatively simple . . . just use good old fashioned soap and water—the hotter the water and the stronger the soap the better. If you get rid of the dirt from yourself and your equipment, you get rid of the radiation."[24] Soldiers were to be comforted with the knowledge that humans came equipped with antiradiation tools: "As to the hazard of inhaling particles of matter, the size of the particle is important. The nose filters out almost all particles larger than 10 microns in size."[25] Clearly, there was no cause for any concern.

Our Good Bomb, Their Bad Bomb

Whenever the AEC described American weapons tested in Nevada as nothing to be afraid of, the wording had to tread a fine line. After all, weren't these the same bombs that our enemy, the Soviet Union, possessed? Shouldn't we fear their bombs? The AEC assured us that our bombs posed no threat to anyone who came near the NTS, even as it maintained that the Soviet Union's weapons were so fierce as to require a massive arms buildup and a willingness to engage in nuclear war. Our bomb good, their bomb bad—this was the message publicly articulated by the AEC in the mid-1950s.

Such a counternarrative shows the contentious nature of atomic imagery during the early Cold War era. Even at the peak of Cold War hysteria, the rifts in governmental credibility that would continue to widen during the next ten years were beginning to become visible around the borders of the Nevada Test Site.

The Green Book shows that the AEC was attempting to toe the rhetorical line between our good weapons and their bad ones. In the introduction to the critical section titled "Fallout From Nevada Tests" the distinction is made clear: "Please understand that in the following discussion of radioactive fallout, we are not talking about high-yield A-bombs or H-bombs tested elsewhere. We are not talking about radiation from enemy bombs designed to do the most damage possible. We are talking only about low yield tests, conducted under controlled conditions at Nevada Test Site."[26] Apparently, the Nevada atomic bombs were not the threatening kind; rather, they were a form of the weapon whose dangers could be "controlled."

A February 1955 statement by AEC Chairman Lewis Strauss, accompanying the AEC's official report on fallout from the 1954 Bravo test, claimed, on the one hand, that "only relatively small nuclear explosions are conducted at the Nevada Test Site. . . . The hazard has been successfully confined to the controlled area of the Test Site." On the other hand, and on the same page, Strauss warned, "In the event of war involving the use of atomic weapons, the fallout from large nuclear bombs exploded on or near the surface of the earth would create serious hazard to civilian populations in large areas outside the target zones."[27] This astonishing dualism is a perfectly framed example of the rhetoric of good bomb/bad bomb in action.

The good bomb/bad bomb rhetoric was evident in mainstream American magazines as well. A 1955 *Newsweek* article replied to frequently asked questions about atomic explosions with the best answers that "science can yet give." The first question was "Will nuclear tests in the Pacific and Nevada harm us?" Readers were assured that "Pacific tests cannot hurt Americans; nor is the weaker radioactivity from the Nevada atom tests harmful."[28] The Nevada tests were not only portrayed as "controlled"; they apparently also gave off a different, weaker type of radioactivity. The only real difference in weaponry referred to here is that thermonuclear weapons were tested only in the Pacific, never at the NTS. In reality, the form of radioactivity released by fission bombs did not differ in any way from that produced by fusion bombs, and radioactive fallout from fission bombs, although generated in smaller quantities, was just as deadly as fallout from fusion bombs.

Civil defense pamphlets were advising Americans to keep a Geiger counter in their fallout shelters in case of Soviet attack, but the AEC derided the importance of Geiger counters to the downwinders. "Many persons in Nevada, Utah, Arizona, and nearby California have Geiger counters these days," the Green Book cautioned. "We can expect many reports that 'Geiger counters were going crazy here today.' Reports like this may worry people unnecessarily. Don't let them bother you."[29]

Horrific descriptions of atomic attacks by the bad bomb can easily be found in the mass culture of the late 1940s and the 1950s. In the fall of 1949, the Soviet Union detonated its first atomic weapon. Many urban daily newspapers responded with graphics like one printed in the *Washington Post* on November 17, showing a map of the District of Columbia metropolitan area with concentric circles of destruction radiating out from the center of town, each marked with a brief description of the scale of devastation that those living in the included neighborhoods might expect if the capital were subjected to an atomic raid.[30] These Soviet weapons were city-busters.

Fear of the bad bomb found its way into the service journals as well. Major General Emerson C. Itschner, writing in *Army* in 1958, noted that "nuclear firepower works for both sides, and not exclusively for us. No Cold War planning can overlook the basic enemy capability of striking directly and with devastating force at our civilian populace."[31] A 1955 article in the *Army Combat Forces Journal* bemoaned the fact that such big weapons were aimed at the same targets that were the objectives of lesser weapons in World War II. Nuclear bombs were a "weapon that must devastate five hundred square miles in order to damage a few acres of factory."[32] Colonel George C. Reinhardt reported in the *Marine Corps Gazette*: "The H-bomb can be 'rigged' by special selection of its casing components (cobalt is alleged to be the most awful). A 'rigged' bomb's explosion would emit clouds of neutrons producing radioactivity that would poison thousands of square miles! One eminent scientist has calculated those radioactive effects and reports to the public that 400 such bombs exactly placed could destroy all life, plant, animal, and human, on the surface of the earth."[33]

Soviet bombs were portrayed as so bad that they might force American military commanders into difficult moral dilemmas. The tough survivor we met in the service journal articles might appear different to a commander under combat conditions. In a section titled "The Living Doomed," Lieutenant Colonel Arthur W. Milberg, an instructor at the Command and General Staff College of the Army, posed a chilling scenario:

> Let's say you are the division commander in this hypothetical situation. The enemy has fired a nuclear strike against elements of your division. Corrective action has been taken to restore the situation. Normal blast, nuclear and burn casualties are being treated or evacuated. One of your commanders reports that his film badge and those of about 250 other members of his battle group show exposure to the x roentgens we mentioned (a debilitating dose). This means that these men represent a group of soldiers who are able-bodied at the moment, and who will be for 15 to 20 days more. But after 20 to 25 days they will all be dead. Let's call on that old service school requirement: What are your actions and orders at this time?

Milberg suggests that the men might be sent home to die among their loved ones, or they might be sent on leave from the nearest base to enjoy their last days. But what if "your situation was so tenuous that it required the application of every possible combat means, would you be justified in requiring these men to continue to serve in their parent units? Or would you organize a kamikaze or bonzai type of unit from among the doomed, for executing especially hazardous missions?"[34]

The ease with which the AEC sketched out our good bombs and their bad bombs would be expanded in the late 1950s into a national rhetoric, articulated by the Eisenhower administration. President Eisenhower himself invoked this paradoxical and classically Cold War rhetoric in his remarks about "clean bombs" in the period 1957–1958. As the fear of fallout from nuclear tests rose in the late 1950s, the president used this rhetoric of duality to sell the idea of clean bombs to the American public. Our possession of these good, clean bombs placed us on the moral, or at least the rhetorical, high ground in the Cold War.

In the presidential election of 1956, the Democratic candidate, Adlai Stevenson, took up the issue of fallout. He argued for a test ban, both as a step in the direction of disarmament and in response to the fears of radioactive fallout. The Eisenhower administration, which had been trying to put a smile on the face of the nuclear issue with such initiatives as the "Atoms for Peace" program, responded in a variety of ways to Stevenson's charges about the dangers of nuclear testing; the particular approach that the administration carried beyond the election and into the management of fears about fallout during its second term was the clean bomb campaign. The idea behind the argument for clean bombs was that the United States was designing nuclear weapons that would eliminate fallout completely. The administration claimed that its weapons laboratories had already developed bombs that were 96 percent fallout-free and that therefore these bombs had an inherent moral superiority. In a classic turn of Cold War logic, Eisenhower argued that it was essential to continue weapons testing because only by testing these new designs could we eliminate the dangers that testing had previously posed.[35]

When members of the Eisenhower administration spoke of clean bombs, they were referring to two separate elements: a detonation protocol for the NTS and a weapon design adjustment at the Pacific Proving Ground. For the fission weapons tested at the NTS, fallout was reduced by detonating the weapons at higher altitudes. The majority of fallout produced by smaller, fission weapons was produced when the fireball of the explosion touched the ground and sucked large quantities of dirt up into the cloud created as the fireball cooled. If the bomb was detonated at a sufficiently high altitude, so that the fireball did not touch the earth, the amount of material that would fall out of the cloud and contaminate those downwind was reduced. The AEC assured downwinders that Nevada weapons were tested on towers (and therefore close enough to the earth to touch it) only when there was a scientific demand for instrumentation very close to the explosion. On all other occasions, the tests were conducted with air-dropped weapons that could be detonated at higher altitudes.[36] In the case of the larger fusion weapons, reducing fallout meant reducing the size of the fission trigger necessary to detonate the fusion component, since it was the fission trigger that was responsible for the majority of the fallout.[37] Enemy weapons, it was assumed, would be designed to cause the maximum amount of damage, and so would be detonated closer to the ground to maximize their fallout potential. Thus they would be inherently "dirtier" than our "clean' bombs.

The notion of bombs free of radioactive fallout appealed to Eisenhower, because it would give him the best of both worlds: the testing necessary to maintain nuclear supremacy and prevention of the threat testing posed to the very people it was designed to protect. The president shared his enthusiasm for clean bombs with reporters at his weekly press conference on June 26, 1957. He announced that scientists had already eliminated 96 percent of the fallout in nuclear weapons and would soon have an "absolutely clean bomb." When one reporter asked if there was a possibility that the Russians might also develop clean bombs, a gleam came to the president's eyes: "I don't know of any better question because I asked it myself. I would say this: I would hope that they would learn how to use clean ones—for the simple reason that then at least the bombs used would be specific weapons instead of weapons of general and uncontrolled destruction." Eisenhower's tone at this press conference made it sound as if in some way a clean bomb was a technical advancement, developed by American scientific ingenuity.[38]

Our Secret Bad Bomb

Beneath the rhetoric, in a report published almost ten years to the day before Eisenhower's speech, the roots of dirty bombs were being planted. However defensively the military approached fallout in Nevada, its offensive use as a radiological weapon was fully and quickly appreciated. In a section of the top-secret *Final Report of the Joint Chiefs of Staff Evaluation Board for Operation Crossroads* (JCS), dated June 30, 1947 we can begin to see a reexamination of the bomb emphasizing its importance as a radiological weapon. This section, titled "The Evaluation of the Atomic Bomb as a Military Weapon," includes an assessment of the importance of Test Baker at Bikini Atoll on July 25th, 1946, and it arrives at a critical lesson: "When a bomb is exploded underwater, lethal residual radioactivity assumes an importance greater than the physical damage caused by the explosion. . . . [T]he detonation of a bomb in a body of water contiguous to a city would vastly enhance its radiation effects by creation of a base surge whose mist, contaminated with fission products, and dispersed by wind over great areas, would not only have an immediately lethal effect, but would establish a long term hazard through the contamination of structures by the deposition of radioactive particles."[39]

This effect was among the reasons that "the bomb is pre-eminently a weapon for use against human life and activities in large urban and industrial areas."[40] This report shows that even in the earliest military planning assessments, the spreading of radioactive fallout was considered as a tactic for use against urban civilian populations.

The report went on to offer a vivid psychological portrait of the effectiveness of fallout as a weapon:

> We can form no adequate mental picture of the multiple disasters which would befall a modern city, blasted by one or more atomic bombs and enveloped by radioactive mists. Of the survivors in contaminated areas, some would be doomed to die of radiation sickness in hours, some in days, and others in years. But, these areas, irregular in size and shape, as wind and topography might form them, would have no visible boundaries. No survivor could be certain he was not among the doomed and so, added to the terror of the moment, thousands would be stricken with a fear of death and the uncertainty of the time of its arrival.

As horrible as this description sounds, it was clear that such a disaster might in itself be an effective use of the weapon: "Thousands, perhaps millions, of refugees would rush from the city in panic, breaking down remaining transportation facilities, congesting highways, and creating in their flight new hazards to life. Among the refugees, for the moment unidentifiable from the rest, would be numbers whose contaminated clothing and any other goods they carried could establish in others the fear of dangerous radioactivity, thus creating a unique psychological hazard."[41]

Military planners had a vivid grasp of the powers of this new weapon. They saw that the atomic bomb was most effective as a radiological weapon, capable of poisoning vast areas beyond its immediate effect of blast and heat. Further, military planners quickly saw the obvious possibility of using the atomic bomb as a terror weapon aimed at destroying the enemy's civilian population.[42]

One of the boards set up under the advice of the JCS report was the Joint Advanced Study Committee, which, in a secret 1950 report to the Joint Chiefs of Staff, focused on the use of atomic weapons in warfare. The report asserted that neutralization of an enemy's air superiority was best accomplished by attacking its air bases with "surface exploded atomic bombs, perhaps combined with radioactive materials." The purpose of detonating the bombs on the surface was to maximize their fallout potential; combining these explosions with other "radioactive materials" could only enhance the lethal impact of the fallout.[43]

The agency charged with preparing for atomic warfare with the Soviet Union during this period was the Strategic Air Command (SAC). The commander of SAC from 1948 to 1957 was Lt. General (later General, and then Secretary of the Air Force) Curtis E. LeMay, the architect of the firebombing of Japanese cities in World War II, and a man whose personal style successfully imposed a mode of operation on the institution as a whole. LeMay fought to win, and rules were not especially useful to him when they got in the way of tactics. LeMay's approach to atomic warfare was to hit Russia hard and quick with everything at his disposal (the "Sunday punch"), thus minimizing the threat Russian weapons posed to his own troops and capabilities. Two weeks after the Bravo test, on March 18, 1954, a briefing was given at SAC Headquarters in Omaha, Nebraska, to a group of thirty officers drawn from all branches of the service. Although this briefing represented SAC war planning before it had detailed knowledge or possession of thermonuclear weapons, it reflected the integration into targeting of fallout as a weapon. The optimum SAC war plan revealed in the briefing called for 150 B-36s and 585 B-47s to drop 600–750 atomic bombs on the Soviet landmass in a "drop as you go" system, emphasizing infrastructure targets, with the result (in the impression of one Navy captain present), "that virtually all of Russia would be nothing but a smoking, radiating ruin at the end of two hours."[44]

Throughout the period in which the government publicly minimized the dangers of fallout and then claimed to be working to eliminate fallout from weapons, the military embraced fallout as a military instrument, in some instances integrating it into war planning as the primary effect of nuclear weapons. Far from changing this tactic, the arrival of large thermonuclear devices enhanced it. And with the advent of intercontinental ballistic missiles in the late 1950s, it became strategically possible to cover the entire Soviet landmass with lethal levels of radioactive fallout in less than an hour. The blast effect of the weapons could be used to destroy specific targets of military value while still creating sufficient levels of radioactivity to allow fallout to be the primary impact on the society as a whole.

⫸⫷

The people who lived or who served their country beneath the mushroom clouds of nuclear weapons tests were presented with an alternative image of the bomb. The bomb downwinders and atomic soldiers experienced was not really *clean*. What *was* clean, what *was* sanitized was the image of the bomb that they were shown. The difference between clean and dirty bombs was primarily one of rhetoric.

The delicate distinction between our controlled, clean, friendly nuclear weapons and the Soviet Union's terrifying and poisonous instruments of destruction was a fine line walked throughout the atmospheric testing era by the U.S. government. In popular culture, depictions of atomic warfare continued to be painted in collages of terror and mass deaths at the same time, in the local communities for whom the mushroom clouds were neighbors, the AEC's public-relations efforts created a different, benign image of the bomb. This image formed a counternarrative to the feared atomic weapon: it portrayed a domesticated bomb.

While this rhetoric served to pacify these specific groups for a short time, the imaginary curtain between the fantasy clean bomb and the actual dirty bomb could not be sustained for long. As growing numbers of downwinders and atomic soldiers began to develop cancers found to be related to their radiation exposure, the veneer began to peel away from the Disney bomb. The cultural schizophrenia made visible through examination of this bifurcated good bomb/bad bomb rhetoric would become more apparent, and it would come to dominate the political discourse in the coming era.

6

The Atomic Kid:
American Children vs. the Bomb

> The first graders . . . learned to spell "atom"
> and "bomb" before they learned "mother."
>
> *Mrs. Elise E. Beiler, teacher,*
> *Indian Springs, Nevada (1952)*

Alone in the Flash: Training Children to Survive an Atomic Attack

As the United States embarked on a furious program of weapons testing in response to the acquisition of nuclear weapons by the Soviet Union in late 1949, there was one group of model citizens who had a more specific understanding of what to expect from the frequent detonation of atomic bombs in the Nevada desert: the students of the Indian Springs School in Indian Springs, Nevada. *Collier's* magazine showed Americans into the two-room schoolhouse that was located in "a converted supply room at the Indian Springs Air Force Base, a security area attached to the closely guarded atomic testing grounds. The children have witnessed four atomic blasts in the last few weeks. Some of the children have seen as many as a dozen of the atomic test detonations" (fig. 13).[1]

A spokesman for the Atomic Energy Commission explained that these children were models for the rest of America's youngsters: "The children in this school by their sheer proximity to the tests are getting the same type of psychological indoctrination we are giving some of our combat troops. If all the school children in the nation could witness an A-bomb blast, it would do much to destroy the fear and uncertainty which now exist." Mrs. Nevin Bartley, one of the two teachers at the school, offered her own assessment: "It's difficult keeping one jump ahead of these Atomic Age youngsters."[2]

The Cold War was a very different experience for American kids than it was for their parents.[3] The parents felt it as a threat to the American way of life, to their health and well-being and those of their families. The children were threatened by the loss of a future they could grow into and inhabit, by the knowledge that they might be the last children on the earth.

Collier's, June 21, 1952

A IS FOR ATOM

13. Students prepare for atomic attack near the Nevada Test Site in a 1952 *Collier's*.

Fear of and preparation for nuclear war were pervasive in American society as the Cold War took hold. With a belligerent enemy in possession of nuclear weapons at the beginning of the 1950s, the decade was gripped by frightening realities. Massive government efforts to design, construct, and deploy nuclear weapons helped to fuel the emergence of what Dwight Eisenhower would later call the military-industrial complex.[4] Historian Michael Scheibach has pointed out another critical element of American Cold War society: "educators, government officials, and parents realized the necessity, even the urgency, of preparing the country's youth for a new, more precarious world. This required information about the atomic bomb itself and its political and social implications."[5]

This generation's children were not the passive, blank slates their adult guardians imagined, however. They were born into a continuum of both American and human culture that carried its own stories. In the United States, that tradition had to do with presenting Americans as the good guys, fighting wars fairly for noble causes. Tom Engelhardt has called this heritage of a triumphalist narrative "victory culture." As he points out, the narrative of the Good War and the narrative of the new Cold War did not fit together seamlessly. "The question of whether or not to use triumphal weapons of a suicidal nature to accomplish national ends proved deeply unsettling not just for adults planning global strategy, but also for children experiencing both the pride of parents returning victorious from the world war and the fear that that war's most wondrous weapon engendered."[6] Engelhardt argues that this tension had unforeseen and profound effects on the baby boomer generation: "If the story of victory in World War II was for a time endlessly replayed in the movies, in comics, and on television, other cultural vistas were also opening up for the young, ones that led directly into whatever terrified grown-ups. To escape not into the war story but into places where that story was dissolving held unexpected pleasures, not the least of which was the visible horror of adults at what you were doing. . . . Many children instinctively grasped the corrosiveness of the postwar transformation, gravitating toward new forms of storytelling that seemed to rise unbidden from alien worlds."[7] In Engelhardt's view, the children of the 1950s "grasped the pleasures of victory culture as an act of faith, and the horrors of nuclear culture as an act of faithless mockery."[8]

Among the most existential documents to reach the American public during the 1950s was a text aimed at children and produced by the U.S. government. This was the famous *Duck and Cover* movie and accompanying pamphlet, produced on behalf of the U.S. government and distributed by the Federal Civil Defense Administration (FCDA).[9]

The historian Margot Henriksen argues that "civil defense films . . . suggested that much of America's psychological trouble was related to the bomb." Of course, it is also true that civil defense films helped to generate such psychological distress.[10] In recent years, *Duck and Cover* has become a classic of comedy and camp, thanks largely to the inclusion of clips from it in the 1982 documentary *The Atomic Café*.[11] But in its original release, the film was deadly serious. *Duck and Cover* was part of the massive, sometimes hysterical, response on the part of the people and the government of the United States to the Soviet Union's acquisition of nuclear weapons and the first Soviet test detonation in late 1949.[12] Should the Soviets launch an atomic attack without warning, children would need to know what steps to take to survive. The purpose of *Duck and Cover* was to teach children how to survive a nuclear attack by themselves, without adult assistance.

Made by Archer Films under contract to the FCDA, *Duck and Cover* would be shown in thousands of schools across the United States, and the companion pamphlet would be distributed to millions. The film came complete with a cartoon mascot, Bert the Turtle, and a catchy theme song written by the same team whose jingle urged Americans to "See the U.S.A. in Your Chevrolet."[13]

The film opens with a cartoon segment featuring Bert the Turtle, who is walking along accompanied by his theme song. Bert walks by a monkey hanging out of a tree, holding a twig from which hangs a stick of dynamite that dangles menacingly close to Bert (fig. 14). Ever alert, Bert sees the danger and drops to the ground, withdrawing into his protective turtle shell. But even in this short cartoon, which is the part of *Duck and Cover* most frequently reproduced and ridiculed, the iconography is a bit skewed: Bert, with whom the kids are supposed to identify, is drawn almost as an old man with a bow tie, a wrinkled neck, and a civil defense–style helmet, while the monkey is drawn as a classically mischievous kid. Even Bert's voice sounds like an old man's.

The narrator tells us that Bert is always prepared for danger, and that's why he has his shell—"Sometimes it even saves his life!" Children have to learn to be safe, like Bert; they have to learn to duck and cover, as Bert does in his shell, to avoid danger. Immediately the narrator turns his attention to the bomb: "We all know the atomic bomb is very dangerous. Since it may be used against us we must be ready for it."[14] In order to make this threat normative, the narrator describes other dangers that the children are more familiar with, such as fires and automobile accidents. There are methods for avoiding or responding to each of these dangers, but the introduction to the effects of the bomb is truly grim:

> Now we must be ready for a new danger, the atomic bomb. . . . You will know when it comes. We hope it never comes, but we must be ready. It

14. Bert the Turtle and the bad monkey in the 1951 civil defense pamphlet *Duck and Cover.*

looks something like this: There is a bright flash! Brighter than the sun! Brighter than anything you have ever seen! If you are not ready and did not know what to do, it could hurt you in different ways. It could knock you down hard, or throw you against a tree or wall. It is such a big explosion it can smash in buildings and knock signboards over and break windows all over town. But if you duck and cover like Bert, you will be much safer. You know how bad sunburn can feel. An atomic bomb flash can burn you worse than a terrible sunburn.

Next the young audience is presented with the basic rationale for their training: there are two kinds of attacks, those with warning and those without, and they need to know what to do in each case. If there is warning, "there will be time for us to get in our homes, schools or some other safe place." In such a case, adults may be present to help the children. The children are told that we can expect to have warning of most attacks from our national defense officials and our warning systems. The narrator then recites a list of the typical places where youngsters might find themselves when they hear the warning sirens—places that until now had certainly seemed to be the safe, idyllic settings of childhood: "You may be in your schoolyard, playing, when the signal comes. That signal means to stop whatever you are doing and get to the nearest safe place fast. Always remember, the flash of an atomic bomb can come at anytime, no matter where you might be. You might be out playing at home when the warning comes. Then be sure to get into the house fast, where your parents have fixed a safe place for you to go."

By this point, many of the millions of children anxiously viewing the film must have realized that their parents had not prepared a "safe place" for them to go when the sirens sound. And then the narrator further deconstructs the safe world of childhood: "Sometimes, and this is very, very important, sometimes the bomb might explode without any warning. Then, the first thing we would know about it would be the flash, and that means duck and cover fast! Wherever you are! There's no time to look around and wait!"

The children are then treated to a demonstration of how to duck and cover in the school hallway. Ducking and covering means taking shelter against any kind of structure in the nearby environment: falling to the ground next to a curb, crouching next to a wall, then covering your head and the back of your neck to shield them from injury. The narrator assures the children that they will be safe if they crouch down and lean against a wall, even though just a minute earlier he had told them that the atomic bomb can "smash in buildings." The youngsters are told to cover their faces and necks, so that "if the glass breaks and flies through the air, it won't cut you," as the camera shows their backs exposed, hardly inspiring a deep sense of safety from flying glass.

It is even possible that "you might be eating your lunch when the flash comes." But a quick dive under the cafeteria table will solve that problem. "Then, if the explosion makes anything in the room fall down, it can't fall on you"—anything, that is, except for the building itself.

Next we meet Paul and Patty in the living room of their handsomely furnished suburban home, where their mother stands waiting for them at the door. She takes each of their hands and kisses them good-bye. They look cheerful as they head out. "Good-bye!" she calls after them. They are now on their own on the front lines of the Cold War, ready to face the Russian nuclear weapons. "Getting ready means we must all be able to take care of ourselves," the narrator explains. "The bomb might explode when there are no grown-ups near. Paul and Patty know this and they are always ready to take care of themselves."

Once Paul and Patty leave home, events begin to unfold. "Here they are on their way to school on a beautiful spring day. But no matter where they go or what they do, they try to remember what to do if the atomic bomb explodes right then!" Then a flash is seen. "It's a bomb! Duck and cover!"

Next we see Tony; he is riding his bike to a Cub Scout meeting when suddenly there is a bright flash. Tony instantly dives from his bike into the gutter next to the curb, "Tony knows the bomb can explode any time of year, day or night, he is ready for it. It's a bomb! Duck and cover! That-taboy Tony—that flash means act fast! . . . Tony knew what to do. Notice how he keeps from moving or getting up or running? He stays down until he is sure the danger is over."

Next, a sudden flash in a crowded school bus. The children duck and cover toward the aisle and away from the bus windows because "the glass may break and fly through the air and cut you." In a school corridor, in a school cafeteria, on a school bus, at a picnic, playing at home or in the park, bright flash after bright flash turn all the normal settings of the daily lives of children into the ground zero of an atomic attack.

While children were supposedly being trained to physically survive an atomic attack, *Duck and Cover* also delivered a subtle message about survival and about the relationship of children and their world to the world of their parents. "Older people will help us, like they always do. But there might not be any grown-ups around when the bomb explodes," the narrator advises somberly. "Then you're on your own." *Duck and Cover* was designed to teach children that they could survive a surprise nuclear war even in the absence of adult caretakers. This message gave young people a powerfully mixed assurance. The film leaves no doubt that the threat of attack is always imminent and that the key to a child's survival is a constant mental state of readiness for nuclear war: "No matter where we live, in the city or the country, we must be ready all the time for the atomic bomb. . . . Yes, we must all get ready now so we know how to save ourselves if the atomic bomb ever explodes near us." But the film also reveals that the world children take for granted, the safe world of their childhood, could dissolve at any moment. And when that debacle happens, the adults will be gone; the youngsters will be on their own.

This is the narrative about nuclear war, about the Cold War, and about childhood that millions of American children, the baby boomers, received from their government and from their teachers in their schoolrooms. *Duck and Cover* told a tale of a dangerous present and a dismal future. Training children much as it was training soldiers, the government used this narrative to portray the world of the baby boomers' parents as unsafe, undesirable, and ultimately unreliable. Ducking and covering is, after all, a catastrophic pose, one in which the emphasis is on avoiding head injury at the expense of bodily injury: it is the desperate posture of an attempt at bare survival. To duck and cover is to fall to the ground and hope that you live to stand back up. As we watch each setting of childhood succumb to the bright flash of death and destruction in the film, no grownups are in sight; it is up to the children to survive the world that their parents have made for them—a world seemingly without a future, where survival is measured day to day, minute to minute.[15]

Duck and Cover presents a vision of a dangerous world that could dissolve at any time yet masquerades as the safe and familiar world of school and friends and family. It projects a world in which such authority figures as teachers and parents, those models of the self as an adult, are ineffective in either protecting the child or providing any continuity between the relatively safe world of the present and that of a future worth growing up to inhabit.

Soldiers in the Cold War

If parents couldn't be present to help their children to survive, at least they could organize to identify their bodies. Starting in 1951, many metropolitan areas issued dog tags to students, and over 2.5 million tags were distributed in public and private schools in San Francisco, Seattle, Philadelphia, and New York City. Federal Civil Defense Administration (FCDA) education experts chose dog tags after considering tattooing, the marking of clothes, and fingerprinting. The tags were intended to aid in the identification of children after the war, helping to reunite them with their families. The heat- and corrosion-resistant metal tags that were chosen could also aid in the identification of bodies after a nuclear attack.[16] In 1981 Albert Furtwangler, a professor of English, recalled growing up in the early 1950s in Seattle: "In fifth and sixth grades, I also dressed every morning with a bit of cold metal against my chest—a dog tag with my name and address, furnished at cost by the Parent–Teacher Association."[17] The military-style tags served to further signify to American children that they were soldiers in the Cold War.

At about the same time, Encyclopedia Britannica Films released a film similar to *Duck and Cover*, titled *Atomic Alert*, for distribution in elementary schools.[18] Like *Duck and Cover*, it was aimed at training elementary-school children to be prepared for nuclear attack. The fact that both films were shown to children in their classrooms served to give these messages a chilling authoritativeness.

15. Prudent teenagers wisely discard their contaminated clothes as they head for shelter in the Encyclopedia Britannica film *Atomic Alert* of 1951.

The film begins by laying out the role of elementary school children in atomic-age America: "The chance of your being hurt by an atomic bomb is slight, but since there is a chance, you *must* know how to protect yourself. . . . We have the national defenses to intercept an enemy, and we all form a team to help each other through emergencies. *You* are on that team."

The two national-defense team members who guide the children through the rest of the film are Ted and Susie. Like Paul and Patty, Ted and Susie help to answer the central question the film poses to its viewers: "What is your job?" Ted and Susie are home alone when the warning of an enemy attack comes. With Ted as the responsible older brother and Susie as the impish grade-schooler, we learn that survival is the primary job of young defense-team members and that survival depends on thorough preparation and practice. "If you're home," the narrator intones, "you've got work to do." Ted and Susie go through a series of checks in the house, from closing the curtains to shutting off the stove and oven (turning off the burners but unwisely leaving the gas line itself open). The radio tells them that this alert is only a test, and when Susie wonders why they have to check everything if it is only a test, Ted lectures her: "We need this practice. Now come on, let's do our jobs." Then they take shelter in their well-prepared basement and check on the supplies they have stashed.

But, the narrator ponders, what if there was a bomb detonation without warning? "What is your job then?" *Atomic Alert* shows children responding to a number of outdoor situations in which, much as in *Duck and Cover*, a flash is followed by the alert actions of children. They take cover inside school buildings during recess; they run into apartment buildings when they are playing outside. They are even told that they should just knock on the door of any house if they are far from home and that strangers will admit them. They are shown jumping into ditches if they are in fields, discarding their outer (presumably contaminated) clothing as they run (fig. 15).

Benefiting now from all of their practice, Ted and Susie turn on their battery-powered radio as they shelter in their basement and hear the civil defense announcer claim that a bomb has exploded between "Fourteenth Street and the waterfront"; then, suddenly, the announcer shouts that another bomb has exploded underwater at the waterfront and that radioactive mist is falling on the city. Ted tells Susie what to do if the mist were to fall on her. They are interrupted by a knock on the door as the local civil defense block warden arrives with a radiation monitor to check the house. The warden's deadpan tone lets the children know that all is in order and under control. He tells Ted and Susie that he has seen their mother at the shopping center and that their father is down at headquarters, so that the kids know that the adult members of their family defense team are doing their jobs. Then he tells the children, "You've done a good job." These little soldiers in the Cold War have done their part to help the team and to defend the nation.

Part of the civil defense narrative was the rapid restoration of social order following an atomic attack. While U.S. government films about the bombing of Hiroshima and Nagasaki would dwell endlessly on flattened and depopulated images of the two cities, civil defense texts dared not envision a devastated American landscape following a nuclear war. Rather, social recovery was to follow a nuclear attack in a natural and controlled fashion. In both *Duck and Cover* and *Atomic Alert*, adult civil defense workers show up quickly once the children have taken the proper steps to insure their own survival.

But most youngsters knew that this scenario was not what they could really expect—for that, they turned to science fiction books and magazines.[19] In Dean Owen's novel *The End of the World*, for example, survivors of a nuclear war have to kill each other to continue to survive.[20] While civil defense authorities, teachers, and even presidents might

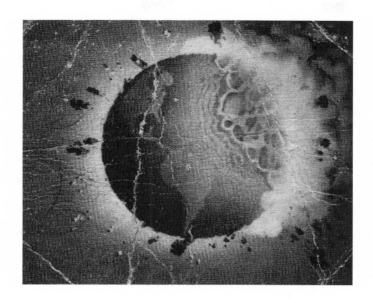

16. Children's collector card "Atomic Doom," part of the Bowman's *Wild Man Picture Card* series, 1950.

describe nuclear war as something that could be won, or that would be followed by the rapid restoration of social order, children heard a competing message loud and clear: their science fiction magazines convinced them that no such comforting illusions should be harbored, and that they would be just as alone after the war as they where when the bombs went off. The flash would not merely mark the interruption of an afternoon of play; quite possibly it would bring the end of the world.

No Future

In 1950, the Bowman Gum Company of Philadelphia, one of America's best-selling baseball-card companies, issued its first series of Wild Man Picture Cards, which were sold alongside baseball cards in candy stores, five-and-dimes, and other shops across America. Card #34 was named "Atomic Doom" (fig. 16). It asked children: "What will a war be like—if it comes? Science is constantly increasing the destructive power of the atomic bomb. In a future war, not one or two but many of these weapons could be let loose on target areas." The results, the card assured, would be catastrophic: "Explosions might cause a chain reaction destroying the earth or rendering it so barren that it could not support human or animal life." The picture on the front of the card showed the earth exploding. The cards came with a stick of gum to chew on.

In the 1952 film *Atomic City*, young Tommy plays with a friend on the living-room floor while his mother is cooking in the kitchen. Tommy asks his friend, "What do you want to be if you grow up?" Tommy's mom is noticeably startled and insists, "*When* you grow up, not *if, when!*" This scene frames a dilemma central to the childhood of many baby boomers: would the world be there when they grew up?[21]

Nuclear fears were very real to American children in the early Cold War years. In an article in the *Bulletin of the Atomic Scientists*, Robert Musil recalled his childhood in the suburbs of New York City: "My first recognition of danger came from the newspapers in the early 1950s. Each year I watched bemused as widening circles, representing atomic destruction on a map of New York crept outward from Manhattan. Only with the advent of deliverable Russian thermonuclear weapons in the mid-1950s did those circles finally reach my home. I began to worry."[22]

Richard Rhodes, who would go on to write the Pulitzer Prize–winning *The Making of the Atomic Bomb*, remembers writing this haiku as a fifth grader in the late 1940s:

Look up in the sky.
See the pretty mushroom cloud.
Soon we will be dead.[23]

During the late 1970s, the journalist Michael Carey worked with the psychiatrist Robert Jay Lifton to collect oral histories of baby boomers' recollections of their nuclear fears in childhood. In another article in the same edition of the *Bulletin of the Atomic Scientists* in 1982, Carey presented some of the results of his interviews that led him to conclude that the bomb had permanently marked this generation. One respondent from Philadelphia remembered that when, as a youngster, he had been "told the United States was a melting pot, one of my thoughts was, 'It really will be a melting pot' because of that business with the bomb." Carey himself recounted growing up in Fairbanks, Alaska, near a Strategic Air Command base, busy with the comings and goings of bombers laden with nuclear weapons. "My school had unsettling air raid drills, but I recall more vividly my terror of the citywide blackouts, when we had to cover our windows with blankets to ensure no enemy could find Fairbanks. I was curious about the bases by day but frightened of the bomb by night."[24]

Another of Carey's respondents recalled seeing film footage of civil defense experiments conducted at the Nevada Test Site when he was a child. One of these showed a house, the famous House One, bursting into flames and exploding from test shot Annie on March 17, 1953: "I mean the thought of a building bursting into flames in that way is kind of startling. . . . It undercuts the sense of reality. You kind of grow up knowing that certain things are stable. I mean that certain presuppositions about the way things are remain constant. Namely, buildings stand. They may burn down or let's say in an earthquake, they might collapse, but reality is fairly stable. When you suddenly see a picture like that, it's kind of like getting the rug pulled out."[25] Another respondent told Carey of a terrifying moment in his childhood in California in the 1950s. He heard a missile test being conducted at one of the many military bases in the area, and he believed that an actual nuclear explosion was in progress. "He dived behind the couch, yelling 'Get down! It's happened!' only to discover that he had made a fool of himself."[26] In his book on the 1960s, the historian Todd Gitlin recounts a particularly gruesome practice in his grade school: "Every so often, out of the blue, a teacher would pause in the middle of class and call out, 'Take cover!' We knew, then, to scramble under our miniature desks and to stay there, cramped, heads folded under our arms, until the teacher called out, 'All clear!'" (fig. 17).[27]

17. Students practice ducking and covering to survive atomic attack in their school in the early 1950s.

How much do we really know about the thoughts of children at the time, as opposed to their later memories? How seriously did children take the presence of nuclear weapons looming between themselves and their imagined futures? During the early 1960s, several researchers set out to answer such questions. Under the direction of Milton Schwebel, a professor and the chair of the Department of Guidance and Administration in the School of Education at New York University, researchers interviewed thousands of public-school students, most of them enrolled in high schools and junior high schools in New York and Pennsylvania; these interviews were held in the immediate aftermath of both the Berlin crisis of 1961 and the Cuban missile crisis of 1962. The interviewers asked students to answer three questions: "Do I think there is going to be a war?"; "Do I care? Why?"; and "What do I think about fallout shelters?"[28]

Schwebel reported a broad range of responses, with students roughly split on whether or not there would be a war. Almost all students, however, said that they did care very much whether or not there was war.

Among the reasons they offered for this concern were: "I will die; my parents, brothers, sisters, friends will die"; "My family and I will be separated"; "If my family dies and I live, I'd rather be dead"; "I am young and want a future to live, marry, have a family, work, create, paint. . . . Even if I survive, what will there be worth living for, with millions dead?" Some students revealed an intense personal anxiety about the future: "I worry. I cry. Sometimes I am disturbed at night."[29]

The work of Sibylle K. Escalona, a professor of psychology at the Albert Einstein College of Medicine, showed data that are much more intriguing. Escalona's open-ended questions about the future, put to 311 children between the ages of ten and seventeen from the New York City area in 1962, reaped some fascinating answers to the question, "Think about the world as it may be ten years from now. What are some ways it might be different from today?" Seventy percent of the youngsters spontaneously raised the issue of war. Of these 219 respondents, Escalona claims, most spoke in pessimistic terms of war as a fairly strong probability. "Maybe we will not even be here ten years from now,' posited one twelve-year-old. "Maybe there will be no such thing as a world." Another child responded, "I think I would be all broken up because of the war which will come. The war destroys New York." One fourteen-year-old said, "The people of the world never change, but the atomic powers will still be expanding and the threat of war and complete destruction will hang as a cloud of fear over the world."[30]

Schwebel's interviews put the notion of war into the heads of the students he interviewed, allowing them to respond positively or negatively to this suggestion by an adult. But Escalona's open-ended questions allowed the students to individually prioritize their own beliefs about the future.

Kids to the Rescue

The baby boomers, taught by their government, their teachers, and their parents to prepare for death and destruction at every waking moment, still managed to find ways to grow up believing in a future. From ducking and covering on the way to Scout meetings to reading about superheroes bitten by radioactive spiders, boomers inhabited a different world from the one in which their parents lived. Where their parents saw a world of fear and threats, these children walked in an unstable landscape filled with heretofore unimaginable possibilities.

"The flash could come at any moment!" cautioned Bert the Turtle. Robert Musil recalls, "It was with that awful knowledge—we were not safe at all—that I experienced duck and cover drills, and developed an early disillusionment with, even disdain for, authority."[31] Groomed to survive an atomic attack in isolation and through constant vigilance, these little soldiers played in a million parks across America and dreamed about what the world might be like when they grew up. And when they dreamed, they knew instinctively that if the world were to exist at all, it would have to be very different from the world of their parents. The baby boomers saw the world they were born into as a world of war, as the first half of the twentieth century had seen two world wars. If this militaristic and nationalistic way of life was to continue, only one outcome was logically possible: nuclear war, commonly referred to as World War III— clearly a war of their parents' generation's making—and this war would be followed by . . . nothing. No future. Since their parents did not seem to be working very hard to bring about change, it seemed obvious that if change was going to come, if the future was to be saved, it was up to the next generation, the children, to change the world.[32]

One early indicator of the emerging role of young people as the *saviors* of the future can be seen in science fiction movies. Peter Biskind, a film historian, has written that science fiction films of the early and mid-1950s often depicted a battle between what he calls "cops and docs" to solve the problem posed by the presence of the monster or the alien protagonist of the movie.[33] This plot line was indicative of a larger tension in society between brute force and scientific reason as the saviors that would provide the tools necessary to overcome the dilemmas of the atomic age. But in the late 1950s another tension began to reveal itself, a generational tension. In these films, typified by the 1958 movie *The Blob*, it is teenagers who save the day. These young people are alert to an unnatural threat to human society, but their parents and other adult authority figures refuse to listen to or believe them. It is only by taking matters into their own hands that these heroes both save the earth and also demonstrate to their parents' generation the actions that must be taken in order to preserve a viable future for the human race.[34]

In *The Blob*, a meteor falls to earth in a field near an archetypal American small town. An amorphous pulsating red blob contained in the meteor devours every life form it touches, growing larger and larger with each feeding. The two young heroes of the film, Steve and Jane, are the first to suspect that something is amiss, but the police sergeant is convinced that Steve and Jane and their friends, all driving hot rods, are the

perpetrators of all the troubles. The young people persist in trying to figure out what is killing the townsfolk. In an early scene, they are taken to
the police station, and their parents are called in. "We were just trying to
warn people," Jane cries. "Nobody will believe us."

The monster continues its rampage, and more people are killed. When
the Blob corners Steve and Jane in Steve's father's grocery store, they hide
in the freezer. The monster disappears, but now they have finally seen it,
and again they try to warn the townspeople. Another of the teens calls
the police to tell them about the encounter, but the belligerent sergeant
who answers the phone refuses to believe them: "Is every kid in town in
on this?" he brays. Disgusted, he tells his boss, "You know, I think they
got it in for me, they've heard about my war record and it bugs 'em,"
emphasizing the generational divide between himself and the teens.

Steve organizes the youth: "All right, we tried to do it the right way,
now we're gonna wake this town up ourselves." They gather their hot rods
in the center of town and all of them begin to lean on their car horns.
One of them activates the air-raid siren. Now they have the attention of
the police department and of all the adults in town. In a telling scene,
also revealing the generational divide, an old man is seen jumping out of
bed as he cries, "An air raid! Where is my civil defense helmet?"

All the adults converge on the town center, where they find Steve
standing at the front of the group. "Listen to me!" he cries, "This town is
in danger! We had to make this noise, we had to make it so you'd listen to
us so we could warn you." He turns to the police chief, "Make 'em listen
to me. There is a monster! We saw it in Dad's store, only it's bigger now!"

The street then fills with people fleeing the Blob, which has moved on
to the movie theater, and finally the adults see the monster and realize
that their children have been right all along. But the advancing Blob traps
Steve and Jane inside a diner, along with Jane's little brother (in pajamas
and cowboy hat) and the diner's proprietors. They take shelter in the cellar as the police attempt to kill the Blob by downing a power line onto it.
This action doesn't faze the monster, and the police and parents all hang
their heads, realizing that they can't save Steve, Jane, and the others. But
Steve will not be defeated. The diner is on fire, and while trying to put it
out, he notices that the Blob retreats from the cold spray of the CO_2 fire
extinguisher. He yells to the policemen that the monster hates the cold
and urges them to get more fire extinguishers. Now the police immediately listen to Steve and are able to drive the Blob back, allowing the teen-
age heroes and the others trapped in the diner to escape. The even bigger
adults in Washington, D.C., now listen to the local cops and send forces

to transport the Blob to the Arctic, where it will stay frozen, unable to threaten society any longer.[35]

Here we can see, as early as 1958, the receptivity among the teen audience to the message that the previous generation just didn't get the nature of the threat facing the human race. It is as though *Duck and Cover* had come true—they were on their own.

In the 1960s, as the American baby boomers came of age politically, they began to respond to this "end of the world" culture in several different ways, and I believe that the most important effect of these narratives on the baby boomers was the emergence of an activist culture strongly focused on effecting change in the world for the better—the so-called counterculture and the New Left.[36] The document that marked the beginning of campus political protest in America during the 1960s was the Port Huron Statement, written in 1962. This call to action on American college campuses (so named because it was written in Port Huron, Michigan) was the founding document of the Students for a Democratic Society (SDS).[37] For the next ten years, the SDS was one of the primary organizing vehicles for anti–Vietnam War protests on American college campuses. The Port Huron Statement begins with a reflection about the reason American youth should become activists: "The enclosing fact of the Cold War, symbolized by the presence of the Bomb, brought awareness that we ourselves, and our friends, and millions of abstract 'others' . . . might die at any time." The statement is a call to action to oppose racism and war, and it makes it clear that "our work is guided by the sense that we may be the last generation in the experiment with living."[38]

A childhood in which these Americans were told that this might be the end of the world, that the future might not be there, was a very important factor that led activist baby boomers to try to change the world. Many of them felt that if the world was going to be there when they grew up, it was only going to be because they had worked to change their present society. Many no doubt felt, like the teen-agers in *The Blob*, that the grown-ups would not listen to them when they insisted that something must be done to save the world. In the face of the end of the world, you have a definite incentive to seek alternative visions of the world and to oppose conventional wisdom. Many of these youths felt that the militarism of the Cold War generation had to be changed if it was not to lead to nuclear warfare. They felt that bringing about change was up to them, and so they were emboldened to act.

⇛⇚

As American adults worried that their lives might come to an end in a nuclear war with the Soviet Union, their children watched them and wondered if they had any future on this earth. In a desperate effort to train these kids to survive nuclear war should it come, the adults were inadvertently giving them a different message: the grown-up world might well be insane and could not be counted on in a crisis. If these children were going to survive, if they were going to have a future, have kids of their own, it would have to be by finding a better way themselves.

All of this is evident in the response of the Atomic Kids in the United States to the fatalistic vision of the future presented to them by the adults in their society. When they were faced with catastrophic social destruction, when they were told that they should learn how to throw themselves to the ground and huddle into a gutter and hope that when they got back up the world would still be there, they chose a different path. They examined this vision of the end of the world and decided instead to try on some different beliefs about the world. One of those beliefs was that militarism itself was the problem, not other nations or ideologies, and that their parents just didn't get the danger.

When the beliefs of the previous generation of war-weary parents and militaristic political leaders walled in the Cold War generation with the concrete blocks of the necessity of preparing for nuclear war, these children, much like plants that find a way to grow through the cracks in the sidewalk, found a way to grow into a believable future. They refused to live in the basement shelter of despair and fatalism about nuclear war that was prepared by the generation that preceded them. They grew up and placed flowers in the gun barrels of American militarism and demanded that their government stand down in its imperialistic war in Vietnam. And they had children, too, because they believed the world would be there for their children, even if that world faced monumental challenges. As a generation, the baby boomers did not solve the problems of militarism or the threat of nuclear war, but they did solve the problem of growing up, of surviving into their future and making lives for themselves in spite of the existential despair that they were spoon-fed in their formative years.

Conclusion

The Magical and the Mundane

> A great many people enjoy war.
>
> *Doris Lessing (1987)*

Nuclear weapons have a unique history: introduced to humanity by Harry Truman, arguably the most powerful person in the world, as a harnessing of the "basic force of the universe" to human will, a force that would end war and usher in a new era of peace and prosperity, they threatened futures and haunted nightmares. In a single day they renamed an era. The sheer force of their existence cast doubt on the inevitability of a human future.

This mythic, almost supernatural framing was the way most Americans first encountered the bomb, and it would remain their primary experience of it for many years. Truman and others employed divine rhetoric to describe the bomb: that it was given to the United States by God, that it liberated the elemental forces of nature that powered the sun, and that it ended the war—and might well make war obsolete. But there was a dark and disconcerting shadow to atomic rhetoric: the placing of such power in the hands of political and military leaders. From the wholesale slaughter of World War I, to the orgy of unrestrained capitalism that caused the Great Depression, to the mechanized slaughter and genocide of World War II, human nature had revealed a violent and predatory side that made faith in the wise stewardship of these new powers impossible. Within days of the news from Hiroshima, alongside the celebrations of victory came deep anxiety about what the advent of nuclear weapons meant for the long-term survival of human civilization. To many, it seemed inevitable that these weapons would be unleashed against the people of the world in their own lifetimes.

It is against this background and this tension that nuclear weapons became facts of life. Even those responsible for its design and use in World War II publicly stated that the human race was at a crossroads where a choice would be made about whether the next decades would bring a golden age or the end of the world. Most people did not feel like they were participants in the making of this choice but rather felt themselves and their children to be cast to the wind, along with human destiny. It was a powerless position, but human agency would indeed find avenues of expression in the coming decades.

This initial designation of nuclear weapons as signifiers of social transformation would color nuclear iconography indelibly. Nuclear detonations reset calendars to Year Zero; nuclear targets became Ground Zero, survivors of nuclear war became the Last Man. Nuclear history and culture would encode this rhetorical DNA into its very structure.

In subsequent years, the U.S. government tried to domesticate the imagery of nuclear weapons. To protect its testing program in Nevada, they talked about "clean" bombs and "fallout-free" nuclear tests. These attempts would bump up against more resonant cultural renderings of the impact of the tests. Already seasoned with magic and possessing seemingly apocalyptic powers, these weapons could not be tamed in the minds of the most Americans. While government descriptions of nuclear weapons moved from the fantastic to the mundane, earlier mythic tropes of nuclear weapons continued to resonate in popular culture sources. Indeed, it became easier to believe in giant mutant bugs than it was to believe that nuclear weapons could be "safe."

Science fiction movies and books explored the post-nuclear landscape, a world where social rules no longer applied, and in which the imagined futures contained very few functioning societies. Surviving humans were left to fight an array of radiation-contaminated mutants and genetically distorted animals and bugs. These stories, drawing on the supernatural mythology of nuclear weapons, expressed widespread anxiety over the dangers of radioactive fallout from nuclear testing and became a driving force behind the ultimate banning of atmospheric testing. The fact that science fiction movies expressed a relationship to nuclear weapons that was more believable than the official government declarations and the reassurances of the civil defense literature or Eisenhower's "clean bomb" speeches demonstrates the power of the alchemical narrative of the bomb. People insisted that aboveground testing had to stop because it was easy to believe such testing was invoking a contaminated, dystopic future.

The belief that nuclear weapons were capable of altering the trajectory of the human future was perhaps the most powerful disruption caused by the weapons. Prior to August 6, 1945, it was easily assumed that the human future would be an extension of the present and past. Regardless of the rise and fall of empires and civilization, human history had maintained a continuity. Power may have shifted from group to group, region to region, but the basic form of civilization held strong. And there was a clear and steady progressive direction to recorded history: increasingly sophisticated techniques of agriculture, and then industry, promised a future more highly developed and technologically enabled than the present. Nuclear weapons were at once the ultimate accomplishment of these progressive forces and also the greatest barrier to their continuation. While myths of the end of the world had existed since the written word, and were common to most religious doctrines, these ends were always at the discretion of divine forces. The existence of a human technology capable of accomplishing the apocalypse made the continuity of the past, present, and future suddenly appear to be questionable at best, and doomed at worst.

Popular culture was central to a growing awareness of these dangers, brought about by incidents such as the fallout contamination following the Bravo test in 1954. The accomplishment of a partial nuclear test ban was driven by public anxiety over the increasing fallout load that civilians were being exposed to. The lack of a believable future was a prime motivator for the emergence of the youth culture of the 1960s, although the banning of atmospheric testing removed nuclear weapons from the eyes and minds of many in the youth culture, which focused increasingly on the civil rights movement and the escalating war in Vietnam.

After atmospheric testing was banned in 1963, Americans were not confronted with the presence of nuclear weapons on such an intimate level. When the testing went underground, the giant bugs and mutant humans disappeared. Even so, nuclear weapons have retained their magical pedigree in popular culture. After the Cold War ended, it became safe to love nuclear weapons as savior weapons. Absent for so long from popular culture, with the exception of a burst of nuclear culture scholarship in the wake of the Nuclear Freeze movement of the early 1980s, post–Cold War movies employed nuclear weapons as humanity's salvation from invading aliens (*Independence Day*, 1996) and from approaching asteroids (*Armageddon*, 1998). Video and computer games revived many earlier nuclear sci-fi tropes, such as the dissolution of society after a nuclear war, with survivors roaming an apocalyptic post-nuclear landscape. These survivors not only live in a world in which modern luxuries no longer exist, but are also free from traditional social conventions and behaviors, encouraged to act violently and solely in their self-interest in order to "win."

Since their creation, nuclear weapons have been seen as *special*, as *other*, as *magical*. They have seemed exceptional. They have not had to follow the rules that existed before their arrival, and neither did anything that they touched. This mysteriousness has helped to justify their presence: the magical language is part of their seduction.

Humans succeeded in tickling the tail of the nuclear dragon. It has yielded the knowledge that we sought, but this act has bound us to a historical process: we are now, inextricably, the dragon's dance-partner. Let us hope that this mythic dance will also yield wisdom in the conduct of human society, lest the dance become the Last Dance.

Notes

Introduction: At the Core of the Bomb, Narratives

1. Information on the nature and naming of this experiment can be found in Lillian Hoddeson, Paul W. Henriksen, Roger A. Meade, and Catherine Westfall, *Critical Assembly: A Technical History of Los Alamos during the Oppenheimer Years* (Cambridge: Cambridge University Press, 1993), 340–42; Thomas P. McLaughlin et al., *A Review of Criticality Accidents, 2000 Revision* (Los Alamos, N.M.: Los Alamos National Laboratory, 2000), 74–75; and Richard Rhodes, *The Making of the Atomic Bomb* (New York: Simon and Schuster, 1986), 611–12.

2. U.S. Atomic Energy Commission, *In the Matter of J. Robert Oppenheimer, Transcript of Hearing before Personnel Security Board* (Washington, D.C.: GPO, 1954), 81.

3. John Canaday, *The Nuclear Muse: Literature, Physics, and the First Atomic Bomb* (Madison: University of Wisconsin Press, 2000), 3; see also H. G. Wells, *The World Set Free* (London: Macmillan, 1914). Canaday mentions that the physicist Leo Szilard had read Wells's book before imagining the possibility of chain reaction in 1935.

4. Canaday, *Nuclear Muse*, 6.

5. Dee Garrison, *Bracing for Armageddon: Why Civil Defense Never Worked* (New York: Oxford University Press, 2006), 66–67. See also Arthur Kramish, ed., *Project Sunshine: Worldwide Effects of Atomic Weapons* (Santa Monica, Calif.: The Rand Corp., 1953).

6. My examination of what I call the alchemical narrative is not to be confused with studies of "nuclear narratives" that focus on the narration of the decision to drop the bomb, written by scholars such as John Dower and Peter Kuznick. The narratives this book examines have to do with the construction of nuclear iconography in culture and society and not on the public framing of political decisions. See John Dower, "Triumphal and Tragic Narratives of the War in Asia," in *Living with the Bomb: American and Japanese Cultural Conflicts in the Nuclear Age*, ed. Laura Hein and Mark Selden (Armonk, N.Y.: M. E. Sharpe, 1997), 37–51; Peter Kuznick, "The Decision to Risk the Future: Harry Truman, the Atomic Bomb and the Apocalyptic Narrative," *Japan Focus*, July 23, 2007, japanfocus.org/products/topdf/2479.

7. "Text of Statements by Truman, Stimson on Development of Atomic Bomb," *New York Times*, August 7, 1945, 4.

8. Donald Porter Geddes, ed., *The Atomic Age Opens* (New York: Pocket Books, 1945).

9. Norman Cousins, *Modern Man Is Obsolete* (New York: Viking, 1945), 7–8. This is the expanded Viking Press edition published in October 1945; for the original editorial of the same title see *Saturday Review*, August 18, 1945, 5–9.

10. "One Victory Not Yet Won," *New York Times*, August 9, 1945, D8; italics added.

11. Spencer Weart, *Nuclear Fear: A History of Images* (Cambridge, Mass.: Harvard University Press, 1988), 13, 5; Mark S. Morrisson, *Modern Alchemy: Occultism and the Emergence of Atomic Theory* (New York: Oxford University Press, 2007), 5. Weart describes Soddy as consciously seeing himself as an alchemist, bringing energy and abundance to the world from simple atoms.

12. Weart, *Nuclear Fear*, 421.

13. Paul Boyer, *By the Bomb's Early Light: American Thought and Culture at the Dawn of the Atomic Age* (New York: Pantheon, 1985), xix.

14. Weart, *Nuclear Fear*, 421.

15. Cousins, *Modern Man Is Obsolete*, 7.

16. "Text of Statements by Truman, Stimson," 4.

17. Formally known as the Treaty Banning Nuclear Weapon Tests in the Atmosphere, in Outer Space and Under Water, signed by the United States, the Soviet Union, and Great Britain, and entered into force on October 10, 1963. A full text can be found in Glenn T. Seaborg, *Kennedy, Krushchev, and the Test Ban* (Berkeley: University of California Press, 1981), 302–5. Seaborg was the chairman of the Atomic Energy Commission at the time the treaty was negotiated and signed; he was also the discoverer of plutonium (1941) and a co-winner of the Nobel Prize in Chemistry (1951).

18. Peter B. Hales, "The Atomic Sublime," *American Studies* 32:1 (Spring 1991): 5.

19. Vincent Leo, "The Mushroom Cloud Photograph: From Fact to Symbol," *Afterimage* 13:1 (Summer 1985): 6. See also A. Costadina Titus, "The Mushroom Cloud as Kitsch," in *Atomic Culture: How We Learned to Stop Worrying and Love the Bomb*, ed. Scott C. Zeman and Michael A. Amundson (Boulder: University Press of Colorado, 2004), 101–3.

20. Leo, "Mushroom Cloud Photograph," 10.

21. "264 Exposed to Atomic Radiation after Nuclear Blast in Pacific," *New York Times*, March 12, 1954, 1. Hundreds of U.S. servicemen taking part in the test were also exposed. The Pacific Proving Ground was designated by the U.S. Atomic Energy Commission in 1947.

22. *Gojira*, dir. Inoshiro Honda, prod. Tomoyuki Tanaka (Toho Films, 1954); *The Beast from 20,000 Fathoms*, dir. Eugene Lourie, prod. Jack Dietz (Warner Brothers, 1953); *Killers from Space*, dir. and prod. W. Lee Wilder (RKO, 1954); *Them!* dir. Gordon Douglas, prod. David Weisbart (Warner Brothers, 1954). The original Japanese *Gojira* was released in the United States with additional footage as *Godzilla, King of the Monsters!* dir. Terry Morse, prod. Tomoyuki Tanaka (Toho Films, 1956).

23. See Milton S. Katz, *Ban the Bomb: A History of SANE, the Committee for a*

Sane Nuclear Policy (New York: Praeger, 1986); Lawrence Wittner, *Resisting the Bomb: A History of the World Nuclear Disarmament Movement, 1954–1970*, vol. 2 of *The Struggle against the Bomb* (Stanford: Stanford University Press, 1997), 246–64.

24. All ads reproduced in Katz, *Ban the Bomb*, 78–79, 82.
25. Jonathan Schell, *The Fate of the Earth* (New York: Alfred A. Knopf, 1982), 1.

1. Atomic Familiars on the Radioactive Landscape

Epigraph: Grant Powers, "Patty, the Atomic Pig," *Collier's*, August 11, 1951, 54.

1. *The Incredible Shrinking Man*, dir. Jack Arnold, prod. Albert Zugsmith (Universal Pictures, 1957).
2. Spencer Weart deals extensively with the issue of fallout and radiation in *Nuclear Fear: A History of Images* (Cambridge, Mass.: Harvard University Press, 1988). See also Paul Boyer, *Fallout: A Historian Reflects on America's Half-Century Encounter with Nuclear Weapons* (Columbus: Ohio State University Press, 1998). There is also an extensive literature on the political impact of fallout. Carolyn Kopp argues that the origins of the fallout debate lie in the separations between the sensibilities of different fields, with the scientists most likely to oppose nuclear testing being biologists, whose priorities were very different from those of politicians like AEC chairman Lewis Strauss; see Carolyn Kopp, "The Origins of the American Scientific Debate over Fallout Hazards," *Social Studies of Science* 9:4 (1979): 403–22. See also Allan M. Winkler, *Life Under a Cloud: American Anxiety about the Atom* (Urbana: University of Illinois Press, 1993); Howard Ball, *Justice Downwind: America's Atomic Testing Program in the 1950's* (New York: Oxford University Press, 1986).
3. Ralph E. Lapp, *Kill and Overkill: The Strategy of Annihilation* (New York: Basic Books, 1962), 63; Samuel Glasstone, ed., *The Effects of Nuclear Weapons*, rev. ed. (Washington, D.C.: GPO, April 1962), 614–15.
4. *Them!* dir. Gordon Douglas, prod. David Weisbart (Warner Brothers, 1954). The Trinity test was the first explosion of a nuclear weapon in Alamogordo, New Mexico, in July 1945.
5. This phenomenon governs in *Them!*, *Gojira*, *The Beast from 20,000 Fathoms*, *It Came from Beneath the Sea*, *The Amazing Colossal Man*, and many others. See *Gojira*, dir. Ishiro Honda, prod. Tomoyuki Tanaka (Toho Films, 1954); *The Beast from 20,000 Fathoms*, dir. Eugene Lourie, prod. Jack Dietz (Mutual Pictures, 1953); *It Came from Beneath the Sea*, dir. Robert Gordon, prod. Charles H. Schneer (Universal Pictures, 1953); *The Amazing Colossal Man*, dir. and prod. Bert Gordon (American International Pictures, 1957).
6. Sontag, Dowling, and others interpret the artistic response to the atomic bomb in Freudian terms, much as the social-science community has done. They locate the social violence expressed in the arms race within the personal human subconscious. Sontag believes that one reason for social violence on this scale is the human need to let out cruel and amoral feelings. See Susan Sontag, "The Imagination of Disaster," in *Against Interpretation* (New York: Dell, 1961), 212–28; David Dowling, *Fictions of Nuclear Disaster* (Iowa City: University of Iowa Press, 1987), 3. Further expression of the Cold War as psy-

chological dysfunction can be found in Terrence Holt, "The Bomb and the Baby Boom," *TriQuarterly* 80 (Winter 1990–91): 206–17. Holt writes of the bomb: "It articulates an imaginary pattern of cause and effect in which the potential victims of nuclear weapons, the babies of the boom, are made to seem responsible for their plight. Ultimately, . . . this particular equation of babies with the bomb suggests that the nuclear standoff of the past forty years has answered needs in our culture that we are unwilling to admit, and may be incapable of giving up" (207). Weart also ascribes a fundamentally psychological nature to the imagery surrounding atomic weapons.

7. Sontag, "Imagination of Disaster," 31.
8. "Good morning, gentlemen. Welcome to Frenchman Flats, the land where the giant mushrooms grow," began the final briefing before an atomic test in Nevada in 1957; quoted in Thomas H. Saffer and Orville E. Kelly, *Countdown Zero* (New York: G. P. Putnam's Sons, 1982), 19. Kelly was the founder of the National Association of Atomic Veterans. Trinity was tested on July 16, 1945; Disneyland opened on July 17, 1955.
9. For the best treatment of the opening of Disneyland, see Karal Ann Marling, *As Seen on TV: The Visual Culture of Everyday Life in the 1950s* (Cambridge, Mass.: Harvard University Press, 1994), 86–126.
10. Several of the most important recent studies of the civil defense program, including examinations of the civil defense aspects of the Nevada test series, have focused on the role that civil defense, and the public relations related to tests at the NTS, contributed to the later militarization of ever more sectors of American society and indeed, of everyday life in the United States. See Guy Oakes, *The Imaginary War: Civil Defense and American Cold War Culture* (New York: Oxford University Press, 1994); Laura McEnaney, *Civil Defense Begins at Home: Militarization Meets Everyday Life in the Fifties* (Princeton, N.J.: Princeton University Press, 2000). Kenneth D. Rose argues that the civil defense program must be viewed as a failure in *One Nation Underground: The Fallout Shelter in American Culture* (New York: New York University Press, 2001).
11. There were thirteen U.S. atmospheric tests in 1955, fourteen in 1956, twenty-one in 1957, and fifty-three in 1958; in addition, there were dozens of atmospheric tests by the other nuclear powers during these years, and dozens more U.S. tests conducted underground. See Therese Dennis, "Tests of Nuclear Explosives," in *The Nuclear Almanac*, ed. Jack Dennis (Reading, Mass.: Addison-Wesley, 1984), 304–5.
12. "*Your* Children's Teeth Contain Strontium-90," *New York Times*, April 7, 1963.
13. Cawelti uses the concept of the symbolic landscape to describe the function of the landscape in western films. See John G. Cawelti, *Adventure, Mystery, and Romance* (Chicago: University of Chicago Press, 1977), 193.
14. Leonard Slater, "The World Blew Up," *Newsweek*, February 19, 1951, 25.
15. Test shot Charlie was part of the Tumbler-Snapper series, dubbed "Operation Bigshot" for publicity purposes.
16. "Bigshot," telecast, KTLA, April 22, 1952. These quotes are taken from the soundtrack of the telecast, viewed at the UCLA Film and Television Archive.
17. Chester Heslep, "It Couldn't Be Done—But T-V Men Did It!" *Quill*, July 1952,

7–10. See also Scott Kirsch, "Watching the Bombs Go Off: Photography, Nuclear Landscapes, and Spectator Democracy, *Antipode* 29:3 (July 1997): 227–55.

18. "At Elm and Main," *Time*, March 30, 1953, 58–59.

19. "The Atom: More Mushrooms," *Newsweek*, March 23, 1953, 26.

20. "At Elm and Main"; "Operation Doom Town," *Nevada Highways and Parks*, June–December 1953, 3–17.

21. "At Elm and Main," 26.

22. "Operation Doom Town." The smoldering of the house before it is torn apart demonstrates that the flash hits the house slightly before the blast does.

23. Federal Civil Defense Administration, *2 2/3 Seconds* (Washington, D.C.: GPO, 1953). *Newsweek*'s coverage (accompanied by four frames and claiming that the house blew up in 2 1/3 seconds) reported the survival of the mannequins in the basement shelters; see Leonard Slater, "Greasewood Fires and Man's Most Terrible Weapon," *Newsweek*, March 30, 1953, 31.

24. "Victims at Yucca Flats," *Life*, May 16, 1955, 58.

25. Archie Teague, "Real Folks Find Test Tribe Dead," *Las Vegas Review-Journal*, May 6, 1955, quoted in Michael Uhl and Tod Ensign, *GI Guinea Pigs: How the Pentagon Exposed Our Troops to Dangers More Deadly Than War* (New York: Playboy Press, 1980), 84.

26. There is a street sign in front of the house in the film with the names Elm and Main; see *The Atomic Kid*, dir. Leslie Martinson, prod. Mickey Rooney (Republic Pictures, 1954).

27. Before the development of nuclear weapons, most of the information about the effects of radiation on living organisms was derived from experiments that exposed generations of fruit flies to radiation in order to measure the extent of genetic mutation; this work earned biologist Hermann Muller the Nobel Prize in Medicine in 1946.

28. Jonathan M. Weisgall, *Operation Crossroads: The Atomic Tests at Bikini Atoll* (Annapolis, Md.: Naval Institute Press, 1994), 120.

29. "Bikini: Breath Holding before a Blast—Could It Split the Earth?" *Newsweek*, July 1, 1946, 20.

30. William A. Shurcliff, *Bombs at Bikini: The Official Report of Operation Crossroads* (New York: William H. Wise, 1947), 84–85.

31. Shurcliff, *Bombs at Bikini*, 175.

32. Weisgall, *Operation Crossroads*, 191.

33. "Animals Used in Bikini A-Bomb Tests Reported to Be 'Dying Like Flies,'" *Los Angeles Times*, July 15, 1946.

34. Weisgall, *Operation Crossroads*, 191.

35. "Aboard the Atomic Ark," *Washington Post*, September 25, 1946.

36. Grant Powers, "Patty, the Atomic Pig," *Collier's*, August 11, 1951, 54. Weisgall reports that a letter, supposedly written by Patty on the stationery of Admiral Nimitz, asserted that Patty was not actually aboard a ship that was close to ground zero (*Operation Crossroads*, 355).

37. Richard Gerstell, *How to Survive an Atomic Bomb* (New York: Bantam, 1950).

38. Richard Gerstell, "How You Can Survive an A-Bomb Blast," *Saturday Evening Post*, January 7, 1950, 74. See also William A. Shurcliff, *Operation Crossroads: The Official Pictorial Record* (New York: William H. Wise, 1946), 67.

39. Defense Nuclear Agency, *Shot Galileo: A Test of the Plumbob Series, 2 September 1957* (Washington, D.C.: GPO, 1981), 26; Ball, *Justice Downwind*, 31. This distance was maintained in Nevada for tests of smaller, kiloton-range weapons; frequently, the troops would march through ground zero after the detonations. In the Pacific, troops were stationed only six miles from the much larger, megaton-range weapons tested there; see Kelly, *Countdown Zero*, 111.

40. Federal Civil Defense Administration, *Duck and Cover* (Washington, D.C.: GPO, 1951), 8; see also *Duck and Cover* (Archer Films, 1951). For an interesting assessment of many aspects of the production of the *Duck and Cover* film, see www.conelrad.com/duckandcover/cover.php?turtle=01.

41. U.S. Atomic Energy Commission (AEC), *Atomic Tests in Nevada* (Washington, D.C.: GPO, 1957), 12.

42. AEC, *Atomic Tests*, 2.

43. *Picture Parade*, September 1953.

44. Samuel W. Matthews, "Nevada Learns to Live with the Atom," *National Geographic*, June 1953, 849.

45. See Winkler, *Life Under a Cloud*, 93. These deaths occurred after test shot Harry, known among the downwinders as "Dirty Harry."

46. Jack Arnold, dir., *Tarantula* (Universal Pictures), 1955.

2. Fallout Stories

1. Federal Civil Defense Administration (FCDA), *Facts about the H Bomb* (Washington, D.C.: GPO, 1955).

2. It was, in fact, the undeniable awareness of the thermonuclear component of the Castle Bravo shot that prompted the AEC to finally admit publicly that the Mike shot *had* been thermonuclear; see FCDA, *Facts about the H Bomb*.

3. Herbert York, *The Advisors* (Palo Alto, Calif.: Stanford University Press, 1976), 73–87; Richard G. Hewlett and Jack M. Holl, *Atoms for Peace and War, 1953–1961: Eisenhower and the Atomic Energy Commission* (Berkeley: University of California Press, 1989), 172–75.

4. See the document "Request to Increase Maximum Exposure (EF3/7.3/32cmf)," at www.aracnet.com/~pdxavets/b4519007.gif (accessed August 31, 2008).

5. Hewlett and Holl, *Atoms for Peace*, 172–75.

6. The fallout cloud created by the Castle Bravo shot extended over 200 miles to the northeast of ground zero, creating a lethally contaminated area of 7,000 square miles of the Pacific. The AEC calculated that many of the islanders (who had been located about 100 miles from the epicenter of the blast) were exposed to radiation at levels equal to those who had been 1.5 miles away from the epicenter of the Hiroshima blast. See Samuel Glasstone, ed., *The Effects of Nuclear Weapons* (Washington, D.C.: GPO, 1962), 460–64.

7. Catherine Caufield, *Multiple Exposures* (New York: Harper and Row, 1989), 112–13.

8. *New York Times*, March 12, 1954, 1.

9. The story of the crew of the *Daigo Fukuryu Maru* (its full Japanese name, meaning "Lucky Dragon No. 5") is told in Ralph Lapp, *The Voyage of the Lucky Dragon* (New York: Harper and Brothers, 1958), 55–88. American press cover-

age can be charted in the *New York Times* from March 17, 1954, through Eisenhower's press conference on March 31.

10. "The Active Straw," *Newsweek*, November 12, 1945, 50.
11. David Bradley, *No Place to Hide* (Boston: Atlantic Monthly/Little, Brown, 1948), xiii.
12. "Problems of the Age," *Time*, August 19, 1946, 90.
13. Bradley, *No Place to Hide*, 134–35. The incident happened a month after the conclusion of the tests. Bradley did not amputate the sailor's arm, and there is no further mention of the sailor's health.
14. "Too Hot to Handle," *Time*, November 10, 1947, 82.
15. "'Death Sand' Kills Subtly," *Science News-Letter*, August 5, 1950, 83; "Death Sand," *Time*, August 7, 1950, 50.
16. "The Inside Story," *Newsweek*, November 8, 1954, 17.
17. John C. Clark, as told to Robert Cahn, "We Were Trapped by Radioactive Fallout," *Saturday Evening Post*, July 20, 1957, 19, 69–70.
18. Helen M. Davis, "Hazards of Smog," *Science News-Letter*, May 7, 1955, 299; "Atomic Light on the Desert . . . ," *Newsweek*, March 21, 1955, 31.
19. Paul Jacobs, "Clouds from Nevada," *Reporter*, May 16, 1957, 10–16.
20. *Them!* dir. Gordon Douglas, prod. David Weisbart (Warner Brothers, 1954).
21. See Joyce A. Evans, *Celluloid Mushroom Clouds: Hollywood and the Atomic Bomb* (Boulder, Colo.: Westview Press, 1998); Jerome Shapiro, *Atomic Bomb Cinema: The Apocalyptic Imagination on Film* (New York: Routledge, 2002); Wheeler Winston Davis, *Visions of the Apocalypse: Spectacles of Destruction in American Cinema* (London: Wallflower, 2003).
22. Patrick Lucanio, *Them or Us: Archetypal Interpretations of Fifties Alien Invasion Films* (Bloomington: Indiana University Press, 1987), 1. See also Mick Broderick, *Nuclear Movies: A Filmography* (Northcote, Australia: Post-Modem Publishing, 1988), 6.
23. *Gojira*, dir. Ishiro Honda, prod. Tomoyuki Tanaka (Toho Films, 1954).
24. *Godzilla, King of the Monsters!* dir. Ishiro Honda and Terrell O. Morse, prod. Terry Turner and Joseph E. Levine (Toho Films, 1956).
25. In the movie, fishermen are shown washing up on shore with "strange burns," much like events involving the *Fukuryu Maru*, which drifted into harbor with a crew suffering from radiation sickness. See Yuki Tanaka, "Godzilla and the Bravo Shot: Who Created and Killed the Monster?" *Japan Focus*, japanfocus.org/products/details/1652; Chon Noriega, "Godzilla and the Japanese Nightmare: When 'Them!' Is U.S.," *Cinema Journal* 27:1 (Autumn 1987): 63–77.
26. *The Beast from 20,000 Fathoms*, dir. Eugene Lourie, prod. Jack Dietz (Mutual Pictures, 1953); *It Came from Beneath the Sea*, dir. Robert Gordon, prod. Charles H. Schneer (Universal Pictures, 1953).
27. "Japan Gets Radioactive Fish," *New York Times*, March 17, 1954, 1; "Case of Bikini Fishermen Causes Furor in Japan," *New York Times*, March 28, 1954, E5.
28. Spencer Weart, *Nuclear Fear* (Cambridge, Mass.: Harvard University Press, 1988), 191. In the classic form, scientists and soldiers competed to defeat these monsters; in this case, the scientists led the military. Peter Biskind sees this struggle as the triumph of liberalism over traditionalism; see Biskind, *Seeing Is Believing: How Hollywood Taught Us to Stop Worrying and Love the Fifties*

(New York: Pantheon, 1983), 101–59. In some plots, like that of *The Thing from Another World*, the scientists cannot be trusted, and force is the key to overcoming the threat. Biskind cites this plot as an example of more right-wing thinking. See *The Thing from Another World*, dir. Christian Nyby, prod. Howard Hawks (RKO, 1951).

29. Biskind, *Seeing Is Believing*, 6. See *Tarantula*, dir. Jack Arnold, prod. William Alland (Universal, 1955); *The Black Scorpion*, dir. Edward Ludwig, prod. Frank Medford and Jack Dietz (Warner Bros., 1957); *The Deadly Mantis*, dir. Nathan Juran, prod. William Alland (Universal Pictures, 1957); *Killers from Space*, dir. and prod. W. Lee Wilder (RKO, 1954).

30. *The Fiend without a Face*, dir. Arthur Crabtree, prod. John Croydon (Amalgamated Productions, 1958).

31. Although the relationship of many alien invasions in films to the Soviet threat of this early Cold War period is obvious, the legitimization of this alien threat by radioactivity speaks to more than just the Soviet enemy; it speaks to the enemy at home. See Jodi Dean, *Aliens in America: Conspiracy Cultures from Outerspace to Cyberspace* (Ithaca, N.Y.: Cornell University Press, 1998), 171.

32. *This Island Earth*, dir. Joseph Newman, prod. William Alland (Universal Pictures, 1955).

33. *The Amazing Colossal Man*, dir. and prod. Bert Gordon (American International Pictures, 1957).

34. *Attack of the 50-Foot Woman*, dir. Nathan Hertz, prod. Bernard Woolner (Allied Artists, 1957).

35. *The Day the Earth Stood Still*, dir. Robert Wise, prod. Julian Blaustein (20th Century Fox, 1951).

36. Biskind quotes scriptwriter Edmund North commenting on the Christian motifs: "It was my private little joke. I never discussed this angle with [producer Julian] Blaustein or [director Robert] Wise because I didn't want it expressed. I hoped it would be subliminal" (*Seeing Is Believing*, 152). For an interesting article on religious themes in atomic imagery in country music, see Charles Wolfe, "Nuclear Country: The Atomic Bomb in Country Music," *Journal of Country Music* 6:4 (January 1978): 4–20.

37. *Red Planet Mars*, dir. Harry Horner, prod. Anthony Veiller (United Artists, 1952).

38. "Spy vs. Spy" first debuted in *Mad* in January 1961. Prohias was a Cuban refugee who was unwelcome in Cuba because of his anti-Communist cartoons; see Tom Engelhardt, *The End of Victory Culture: Cold War America and the Disillusioning of a Generation* (New York: Basic Books, 1995), 131.

39. The most obvious example of this is the television show *Star Trek*, with its internationally and racially unified crew.

40. Biskind sees this cosmic viewpoint as leftist (*Seeing Is Believing*, 152–57). See also Andrew Tudor, *Monsters and Mad Scientists* (Cambridge: Basil Blackwell, 1989), 39–47.

41. Howard Ball, *Justice Downwind: America's Atomic Testing Program in the 1950's* (New York: Oxford University Press, 1986), 69–70.

3. Nuclear Approach/Avoidance: Social Scientists and the Bomb

1. Donald Porter Geddes, ed., *The Atomic Age Opens* (New York: Pocket Books, 1945), 174–75.
2. Paul Boyer, *By the Bomb's Early Light* (New York: Pantheon, 1985), 169. Boyer presents a thorough discussion of the movement among social scientists to use the bomb to increase federal funding for social-science projects (166–77).
3. William Fielding Ogburn, *Social Change with Respect to Culture and Original Nature* (1922; repr., New York: Viking, 1950), 3–4.
4. "Atomic Force: Its Meaning for Mankind," *Chicago Roundtable* radio broadcast, August 12, 1945, transcript quoted in Geddes, *The Atomic Age Opens*, 206–21.
5. William Fielding Ogburn, Letter to Harry S. Truman, October 1, 1945, Papers of William Fielding Ogburn, University of Chicago Library. Ogburn would later write: "It is the function of the natural scientist to make the bomb, but of the social scientist to say what the social consequences are likely to be." "Sociology and the Atom," *American Journal of Sociology* 51:4 (January 1946): 267.
6. William Fielding Ogburn, "Memorandum on the Social Implications of Atomic Energy," Ogburn papers.
7. Norman Cousins, *Modern Man Is Obsolete* (New York: Viking, 1945), 11.
8. *Higher Education for American Democracy* (Washington, D.C.: GPO, 1947), 92.
9. Lewis Mumford, "Technics and the Future," reprinted in *Interpretations and Forecasts, 1922–1972* (New York: Harcourt Brace Jovanovich, 1979), 289, 283. See also Casey Blake, *Beloved Community* (Chapel Hill: University of North Carolina Press, 1990).
10. Lewis Mumford, *The Transformations of Man* (New York: Harper and Brothers, 1956), 179. See also Mumford, "Gentlemen, You Are Mad!" *Saturday Review of Literature*, March 2, 1946, 5–6.
11. Louis Wirth, "Responsibility of Social Science," in "The Social Implications of Modern Science," special issue, *Annals of the American Academy of Political and Social Science* 249 (January 1947): 143.
12. Wirth, "Responsibility," 151. See also Talcott Parsons, "The Science Legislation and the Social Sciences," *American Sociological Review* 11:6 (December 1946): 653–66.
13. Hornell Hart, "Technological Acceleration and the Atom Bomb," *American Sociological Review* 11:3 (June 1946): 291.
14. Feliks Gross, "Some Social Consequences of Atomic Discovery," *American Sociological Review* 15:1 (February 1950): 45.
15. David Bradley, *No Place to Hide* (Boston: Atlantic Monthly/Little, Brown, 1948), xiii–xiv. See also Ralph Lapp, *Must We Hide?* (Cambridge, Mass.: Addison-Wesley, 1949).
16. Robert Hutchins, *The Atomic Bomb versus Civilization*, Human Events Pamphlet (Chicago: Human Events, 1945), 13.
17. Robert Hutchins, "1950," *Common Cause* 1:1 (July 1947): 1.
18. Boyer, *By the Bomb's Early Light*, 170. The classic study of the "scientists' movement" of the atomic scientists to influence atomic policy is Alice Kimball Smith, *A Peril and a Hope: The Scientists' Movement in America 1945–47*

(Chicago: University of Chicago Press, 1965). Smith's study barely mentions the social sciences.

19. "Social Psychiatry," *Science News-Letter*, December 1, 1945, 347.

20. Krech was a Swarthmore psychologist and chairman of the committee. David Krech, "Psychology and Atomic Energy," Committee on International Peace of the Society for the Psychological Study of Social Issues, 1946, Papers of the Federation of American Scientists, University of Chicago Library (hereafter cited as FAS); see also Krech, letter of July 26, 1946, FAS. The SPSSI also issued a paper outlining a "five-point plan" to the atomic scientists, which called, among other things, for an understanding that "the atomic bomb danger must be understood by everybody." See "Atom Control Psychology," *Science News-Letter*, June 8, 1946, 359.

21. Watson Davis, "Science for Survival," speech to the Engineers Club of Lehigh Valley, Packard Auditorium, Lehigh University, Bethlehem, Pennsylvania, October 12, 1949, FAS.

22. Bruce Bliven, "The Bomb and the Future," *New Republic*, August 20, 1945, 210–12.

23. Bruce Bliven, "Atomic and Human Energy," *New Republic*, August 27, 1945, 241.

24. Franz Alexander, "The Bomb and the Human Psyche," *United Nations World*, November 1949, 32.

25. Ian Nicholson, "'The Approved Bureaucratic Torpor': Goodwin Watson, Critical Psychology, and the Dilemmas of Expertise, 1930–1945—Society for the Psychological Study of Social Issues' First President," *Journal of Social Issues* 54:1 (Spring 1998): 29. See also Nicholson, "The Politics of Scientific Social Reform, 1936–1960: Goodwin Watson and the Society for the Psychological Study of Social Issues," *Journal of the History of the Behavioral Sciences* 33:1 (Winter 1997): 39–60.

26. The Manhattan Security Project, "A Plan for Research on the Psychological Foundations of Peace," 1946, FAS. In 1946 Joseph H. Willits, director for the social sciences at the Rockefeller Foundation, disagreed: "No social 'atomic bomb' can be produced by social students to neutralize the atomic bomb," he informed the annual gathering of the American Philosophical Society. *Proceedings of the American Philosophical Society* 30:1 (January 1946): 48–49.

27. Manhattan Security Project, "Plan for Research."

28. Ibid.

29. Terence Ball, "The Politics of Social Science in Postwar America," in *Recasting America: Culture and Politics in the Age of the Cold War*, ed. Lary May (Chicago: University of Chicago Press, 1989), 81.

30. Jules H. Masserman, "Mental Hygiene in a World Crisis," speech to the Annual Conference of the Women's Auxiliary of the American Medical Association, November 7, 1947, 11, Papers of the *Bulletin of the Atomic Scientists*, University of Chicago Library (hereafter cited as BAS).

31. Masserman, "Mental Hygiene," 5.

32. Hutchins, *Atomic Bomb versus Civilization*, 8.

33. Hutchins, *Atomic Bomb versus Civilization*, 12–13.

34. Bertrand Russell, "A Guide for Living in the Atomic Age," *United Nations World*, November 1949, 36.

35. Lewis Mumford, "How War Began," *Saturday Evening Post*, April 18, 1959, 24–25.
36. Mumford, "How War Began."
37. Ellen Schrecker, "Cold War Triumphalism and the Real Cold War," in *Cold War Triumphalism: The Misuse of History after the Fall of Communism*, ed. Ellen Schrecker (New York: New Press, 2004), 11.
38. Ball, "Politics of Social Science," 83.
39. Joint Chiefs of Staff, "Final Report of the Joint Chiefs of Staff Evaluation Board for Operation Crossroads," Enclosure D, "The Evaluation of the Atomic Bomb as a Military Weapon." Operation Crossroads was the military name given to the series of atomic tests carried out at Bikini Atoll in 1946. See William A. Shurcliff, *Bombs at Bikini: The Official Report of Operation Crossroads* (New York: William H. Wise, 1947); Jonathan M. Weisgall, *Operation Crossroads: The Atomic Tests at Bikini Atoll* (Annapolis, Md.: Naval Institute Press, 1994).
40. JCS 1691/3, 89. In April 1951, AEC chairman Gordon Dean advised Truman against using the bomb in Korea because its limited effectiveness in mountainous terrain would give the weapons an image of being "psychological duds." Dean diary, April 9, 1951, quoted in Philip L. Fradkin, *Fallout: An American Nuclear Tragedy* (Tucson: University of Arizona Press, 1989), 95.
41. Bernard Brodie, "The American Scientific Strategists," Rand paper P-2979 (Santa Monica, Calif.: The RAND Corporation, October 1964); see also Alex Abella, *Soldiers of Reason: The Rand Corporation and the Rise of the American Empire* (Orlando, Fla.: Harcourt, 2008); Sharon Ghamari-Tabrizi, *The Worlds of Herman Kahn: The Intuitive Science of Thermonuclear War* (Cambridge, Mass.: Harvard University Press, 2004); Bruce L. R. Smith, *The RAND Corporation* (Cambridge, Mass.: Harvard University Press, 1966). RAND stands for "research and development" and is based on the colloquial shorthand "R and D."
42. Gregg Herken, *Counsels of War* (New York: Alfred A. Knopf, 1985), xiii–xvi. See also Fred Kaplan, *The Wizards of Armageddon* (New York: Simon and Schuster, 1983), 51–73.
43. "The Atomic Dilemma," *Annals of the American Academy of Political and Social Science* 249 (January 1947): 32. See also Bernard Brodie, "War in the Atomic Age," in *The Absolute Weapon*, ed. Bernard Brodie (New York: Harcourt Brace, 1946), 21–69.
44. Brodie, *American Scientific Strategists*, 20. Herken notes that many of RAND's early researchers were recruited at an economics conference in New York City in 1947; see Herken, *Counsels*, 74.
45. Herken, *Counsels*, 341.
46. Irving L. Janis, "Psychological Aspects of Vulnerability to Atomic Bomb Attacks," Memorandum for RAND Corporation, Crisis and Disaster Study (January 15, 1949), FAS.
47. Irving L. Janis "Psychological Problems of A-Bomb Defense," *Bulletin of the Atomic Scientists* 6:8 (August–September 1950), 256–62; see also Irving L. Janis to Clyde A. Hutchinson Jr., July 6, 1950, BAS. An example of a silly RAND psychological analysis can be found in Fred Charles Ikle, *The Social Impact of Bomb Destruction* (Norman: University of Oklahoma Press, 1958), where Ikle—drawing on an idea expressed by Jacob Burckhardt, the famous historian

of the Renaissance—speculates that "the enormous loss of works of art from nuclear bombing destruction" might actually lead to "a less encumbered creation of new art" in a postwar civilization (227).

48. Janis, "Psychological Problems of A-Bomb Defense," 257.

49. For discussions of the civil defense literature, see Laura McEnaney, *Civil Defense Begins at Home: Militarization Meets Everyday Life in the Fifties* (Princeton: Princeton University Press, 2000); Kenneth D. Rose, *One Nation Underground: The Fallout Shelter in American Culture* (New York: New York University Press, 2001).

50. Dale C. Cameron, "Psychiatric Implications of Civil Defense," *American Journal of Psychiatry* 106 (February 1950): 588–89. See also Leonard F. Stevens, "The Care of Psychological Casualties in Atomic Disaster," *American Journal of Nursing* 51:8 (August 1951): 513–14.

51. James P. Cooney, "Psychological Factors in Atomic Weapons," speech before the American Public Health Association, November 12, 1948, Federation of American Scientists papers, University of Chicago Library.

52. Howard Rosenberg, *Atomic Soldiers: American Victims of Nuclear Experiments* (Boston: Beacon Press, 1980), 40–41. See also Ellis A. Johnson to Dr. Detlev W. Bronk, November 11, 1949, papers of the Office of the Provost, John Hopkins University Library; "Address by Lt. General James M. Gavin before the United States Army Educational Advisor's Conference," January 29, 1958, Human Resource Research Office papers, George Washington University Library.

53. Human Resources Research Office (HumRRO), *Desert Rock I: A Psychological Study of Troop Reactions to an Atomic Explosion*, Technical Report 1 (TR-1), Washington, D.C., February 1953; Human Resources Research Office, *Desert Rock IV: Reactions of an Armored Infantry Battalion to an Atomic Bomb Maneuver*, Technical Report 2 (TR-2) Washington, D.C., August 1953.

54. HumRRO, *Bibliography of Reports: As of 30 June 1958* (Washington, D.C.: George Washington University, 1958), 1.

55. The Operations Research Office was established by the U.S. Army at Johns Hopkins University in 1948 and served as the Army's civilian "think tank," much as the RAND corporation did for the Air Force.

56. Rosenberg, *Atomic Soldiers*, 46–48. ORO researchers would come to play a central role in designing Cold War psychological-warfare techniques.

57. HumRRO, *Desert Rock I*, x.

58. HumRRO, *Desert Rock IV*, 52–53.

59. John E. Dahlquist, "We Will Survive If We Have Leadership," *Army*. February 1956, 36; italics added.

60. John T. Burke, "Mind Against Nukes," *Army*, December 1959, 55.

61. Judd Marmor, "Psychological Obstacles to the Peaceful Resolution to the Cold War," in *Behavioral Science and Human Survival*, ed. Milton Schwebel (Palo Alto: Science and Behavior Books, 1965), 57. See also Fairfield Osborn, *Our Plundered Planet* (Boston: Little, Brown, 1948).

62. Committee on Social Issues, "War and the Nature of Man," *Psychiatric Aspects of the Prevention of Nuclear War, Report Number 57* (New York: The Group for the Advancement of Psychiatry, 1964), 229.

63. Robert Jay Lifton, *Death in Life: Survivors of Hiroshima* (New York: Random House, 1967), 32–34.

64. Robert J. Lifton, "Vietnam—Beyond Atrocity" (1971), reprinted in Lifton, *The Future of Immortality, and Other Essays for a Nuclear Age* (New York: Basic Books, 1987), 56–57.

65. Lifton, "Vietnam—Beyond Atrocity," 59.

4. Survival of Self and Nation under Atomic Attack

1. John F. Kennedy, "Speech to the Nation, July 25, 1961," *Papers of the Presidents of the United States: John F. Kennedy, 1961* (Washington, D.C.: GPO, 1962), 533–40. The household warning system never went beyond the planning stages. On the history of the civil defense program see Kenneth D. Rose, *One Nation Underground: The Fallout Shelter in American Culture* (New York: New York University Press, 2001); Guy Oakes, *The Imaginary War: Civil Defense and American Cold War Culture* (New York: Oxford University Press, 1994); Laura McEnaney, *Civil Defense Begins at Home: Militarization Meets Everyday Life in the Fifties* (Princeton: Princeton University Press, 2000).

2. Many civil defense authorities and commentators did directly address the issue of survival in terms of proximity to ground zero. These proponents advocated "dispersal" of urban industries and populations. One of their policy successes was the Eisenhower Interstate Highway system; in maps of atomic attack on cities, the highways' beltway loops around these same urban areas can be seen as the concrete embodiment of the concentric rings of destruction radiating out from city centers.

3. Federal Civil Defense Administration (FCDA), *Survival under Atomic Attack* (Washington, D.C.: GPO, 1950), 3.

4. FCDA, *Survival*, 31. As many as 18 million copies of civil defense pamphlets on first aid after atomic attacks were also distributed in the first half of 1951, see "18,000,000 Civil Defense Pamphlets on First Aid," *Science News-Letter*, July 31, 1951, 34.

5. FCDA, *This Is Civil Defense* (Washington, D.C.: GPO, 1951), 4, 31.

6. FCDA, *What about You and Civil Defense?* (Washington, D.C.: GPO, 1953), 3, 5.

7. FCDA, *This Is Civil Defense*, 10, 4.

8. FCDA, *What You Can Do Now* (Washington, D.C.: GPO, 1952).

9. FCDA, *Facts about the H Bomb* (Washington, D.C.: GPO, 1955), 5.

10. President John F. Kennedy, "A Message from the President, Sept. 7, 1961," *Life*, September 13, 1961, 95.

11. American Council on Education, *Civil Defense and Higher Education* (Washington, D.C.: American Council on Education, 1954), 3.

12. Civilian Protection Group. *Preparing Now for Civil Defense Responsibility* (Washington, D.C.: The Civilian Protection Group, 1950), 1.

13. Rose, *One Nation Underground*, 113–49.

14. Tom Engelhardt, *The End of Victory Culture: Cold War America and the Disillusioning of a Generation* (New York: Basic Books, 1995), 107.

15. This situation was especially true in the narratives of the thermonuclear

period, in which the actual radiation levels from fallout might remain high for several weeks.

16. Richard Gerstell, *How to Survive an Atomic Bomb* (New York: Bantam, 1950), 61, 138–39.

17. "Be Quiet after Explosion," *Science News-Letter*, August 12, 1950, 120. A year later, another expert advised that having pale skin and wearing a "hooded suit resembling a Klansman's robe covered in aluminum foil" was the best defense against the heat of an atomic explosion; see "'KKK' Robe, Light Skin Help Foil A-Bomb Heat," *Science News-Letter*, October 13, 1951, 231.

18. Office of Civil Defense, Department of Defense, *Handbook for Emergencies* (Washington, D.C.: GPO, 1963), 7, 17.

19. Gerstell, *How to Survive*, inside front cover, 11, and back cover.

20. FCDA, *Survival*, 12. Notice this early expression of cold-heartedness toward neighbors.

21. Stuart Cloete, "'The Blast,' Part 2," *Collier's*, April 12, 1947, 19.

22. *You Can Beat the A-Bomb*, dir. Walter Colmes (RKO, 1950); FCDA, *Target You* (Philip Ragan Productions, 1953). *You Can Beat the A-Bomb* was made with the cooperation of the Council on Atomic Implications. Philip Ragan Associates was also involved in the production of the film based on the 1946 book *One World or None*, discussed later in this chapter.

23. *Warning Red*, dir. Nicholas Webster (Norwood Studios, 1956).

24. "Flash of Darkness," *Medic*, dir. John Meredyth Lucas (NBC, February 14, 1955).

25. Herman Kahn, *On Thermonuclear War*, 2nd ed. (New York: Free Press, 1960), 308.

26. Mordecai Roshwald, *Level 7* (New York: McGraw Hill, 1959).

27. Nevil Shute, *On the Beach* (New York: William Morrow, 1957), 235–36.

28. Shute, *On the Beach*, 278.

29. General of the Army Hap Arnold first evoked the image of the push-button war in a press conference three weeks after the bombings of Hiroshima and Nagasaki. See "Push-Button War," *Newsweek*, August 27, 1945, 50.

30. *Panic in Year Zero*, dir. Ray Milland (American International Pictures, 1962).

31. Jack Shaheen points out that in *Panic in Year Zero* "the new beginning is the old belief in technology and the ethos of the gun"; see his "Panic in Year Zero," in *Nuclear War Films*, ed. Jack G. Shaheen (Carbondale: Southern Illinois University Press, 1978), 49.

32. "Gun Thy Neighbor," *Time*, August, 18, 1961, 58. This same sentiment brings up issues of the abandonment of cities as it is depicted in these films, with the racial implications that accompany such ideas in postwar America, as an iconographic theme in civil defense pamphlets. One FDCA pamphlet, *Four Wheels to Survival* (Washington, D.C.: GPO, 1953), clearly shows a family escaping from a city as a means of survival.

33. Margot Henriksen, *Dr. Strangelove's America: Society and Culture in the Atomic Age* (Berkeley: University of California Press, 1997), 205.

34. "Gun Thy Neighbor."

35. "Gun Thy Neighbor." A more sensible response was given by Methodist minister Paul A. Schlipp, professor of philosophy at Northwestern University: "The

immorality takes place much earlier than when people are in their shelters. It occurs when people think they can protect themselves from all-out nuclear war."

36. L. C. McHugh, "Ethics at the Shelter Doorway," *America: A Catholic Review of the Week,* 105:27 (September 30, 1961): 825. McHugh was also an avid believer in extraterrestrial aliens.

37. "Gun Thy Neighbor."

38. McHugh, "Ethics," 826.

39. McHugh, "Ethics," 824–27.

40. "Gun Thy Neighbor."

41. Quote taken from Kevin Rafferty, Jayne Loader, and Pierce Rafferty, *Atomic Café: The Book of the Movie* (New York: Bantam, 1982), 101.

42. "Civil Defense: The Sheltered Life," *Time,* October 20, 1961, 22. Rose asserts that the debate over guns and neighbors in the fallout shelter "would spell doom for a national shelter system"; see *One Nation Underground,* 112.

43. "Shelter Morality," *Commonweal,* Oct. 27, 1961, 109.

44. Rose, *One Nation Underground,* 97; the Kennedy quote is from his address in Los Angeles at a dinner of the Democratic Party of California on November 18, 1961; see www.presidency.ucsb.edu/ws/index.php?pid=8452.

45. Henriksen, *Dr. Strangelove's America,* 214. Scholarship on *The Twilight Zone* includes Gordon F. Sander, *Serling: The Rise and Twilight of Television's Last Angry Man* (New York: Plume, 1994),; Rick Worland, "Sign-Posts Up Ahead: *The Twilight Zone, The Outer Limits,* and TV Political Fantasy, 1959–1965," *Science Fiction Studies* 23 (1996): 103–22; Peter Wolfe, *In the Zone: The Twilight World of Rod Serling* (Bowling Green, Ohio: Bowling Green State University Popular Press, 2000); Don Presnell and Marty McGee, *A Critical History of Television's Twilight Zone, 1959–1964* (Jefferson, N.C.: McFarland, 1998); see also Jeffery Sconce, "The Outer Limits of Oblivion," in *The Revolution Will Not Be Televised: Sixties Television and Social Conflict,* ed. Lynn Spigel and Michael Curtin (New York: Routledge, 1997), 21–45.

46. "The Shelter," teleplay by Rod Serling (CBS-TV, September 11, 1961). See also Sander, *Serling,* 181.

47. John Hersey, *Hiroshima* (New York: Alfred A. Knopf, 1946). Hersey's method, which was to start by introducing characters before describing their experiences with atomic explosions in order to engage readers with the characters, became the standard form for artists who depicted atomic war in novels or film. Examples include Shute, *On the Beach*; *Threads,* dir. and prod. Michael Jackson (BBC Pictures, 1984); and *The Day After,* dir. Nicholas Meyer, prod. Robert Papazian (ABC-TV, 1984). Paul Boyer, *By the Bomb's Early Light: American Thought and Culture at the Dawn of the Atomic Age* (New York: Pantheon, 1985), 203–10, analyzes the reaction to Hiroshima, sensing an almost numb reaction among Americans to Hersey's book. Many critics faulted Hersey for focusing on survivors, arguing that this distracted readers from the fact that the true horrors of the bomb were the numbers it killed. John Leonard sorts out the conflicting reactions to the book in "Looking Back at Hiroshima Makes Uneasy Viewing," *New York Times,* August 1, 1976; see also Michael Yavenditti, "John Hersey and the American Conscience: The Reception of 'Hiroshima,'"

Pacific Historical Review 43 (February 1974): 32–34. See also Patrick B. Sharp, "From Yellow Peril to Japanese Wasteland: John Hersey's 'Hiroshima,'" in "Literature and Apocalypse," special issue, *Twentieth Century Literature* 46:4 (Winter 2000): 434–52.

48. Hersey, *Hiroshima*, 20–21. Hersey's line "a human being was crushed by books" was a clear reference to the destructive power of the highly intellectualized thought that went into the bomb's design and construction. It is the sentence with which Hersey ends his first chapter, in which the explosion occurs.

49. Hersey, *Hiroshima*, 42.

50. *One World or None* (Philip Ragan Productions, 1946). Spencer Weart, *Nuclear Fear: A History of Images* (Cambridge, Mass.: Harvard University Press, 1988), 236.

51. The Wallace Thorsen Organization, *Program for the Emergency Committee of Atomic Scientists* (1946), 18, in the Papers of the Emergency Committee of Atomic Scientists, University of Chicago Library.

52. The Atomic Scientists Report, *The Problem of the Bomb* 4 (1946), radio script in the Papers of the Federation of American Scientists, University of Chicago Library.

53. Robert Littell, "What the Atomic Bomb Would Do to Us," *Reader's Digest*, May 1946, 125.

54. Philip Ragan Associates, Inc., "Proposal for a Ten Minute Animated Film to Be Sponsored by the I.C.C. (*One World or None*)" (1946), 3–4, in the Papers of the Federation of American Scientists, University of Chicago Library.

55. Rodney Baker, *The Hiroshima Maidens* (New York: Viking, 1985), 93.

56. *This Is Your Life*, host Ralph Edwards, NBC (May 11, 1955). See also Robert A. Jacobs, "Reconstructing the Perpetrator's Soul by Reconstructing the Victim's Body: The Hiroshima Maidens in the American Mind," *Intersections: Gender and Sexuality in Asia and the Pacific* 24 (December 2009): forthcoming.

5. Good Bomb / Bad Bomb

1. "Life in These United States," *Reader's Digest*, October 1953, 52.

2. Fred I. Greenstein, *The Hidden-Hand Presidency: Eisenhower as Leader* (New York: Basic Books, 1982). In "Atoms for Peace and Nuclear Hegemony: The Rhetorical Structure of a Cold War Campaign" (*Armed Forces and Society* 23:4 [1977]: 571–93), Martin J. Medhurst shows the calculating Eisenhower carefully laying out his strategic rhetoric in the "Atoms for Peace" program. Robert L. Ivie responds to Robert Divine's revisionist account of Eisenhower as a frustrated peacemaker, casting Eisenhower throughout his presidency as the consummate Cold Warrior whose calculated use of rhetorical strategies amounted to a form of psychological warfare. See "Eisenhower as Cold Warrior," in *Eisenhower's War of Words: Rhetoric and Leadership*, ed. Martin J. Medhurst (East Lansing: Michigan State University Press, 1994), 7–25; and Robert A. Divine, *Eisenhower and the Cold War* (Oxford: Oxford University Press, 1981). See also Richard G. Hewlett and Hack M. Holl, *Atoms for Peace and War, 1953–1961: Eisenhower and the Atomic Energy Commission* (Berkeley: University of California Press, 1989), 335–36.

3. Defense Nuclear Agency, *Shot Galileo: A Test of the Plumbob Series, 2 September 1957* (Washington, D.C.: GPO, 1981), 26; Howard Ball, *Justice Downwind: America's Atomic Testing Program in the 1950s* (New York: Oxford University Press, 1985), 31. In December 1952, responsibility for the safety of troops participating in atomic tests was transferred from the AEC to the Department of Defense. This shift had the effect of raising the permissible radiation exposure for troops and allowing them to be moved closer to the detonation point. See *Troop Participation in Continental Tests*, Report by the Director, AEC Division of Military Application, December 1952.

4. The literature on fallout in downwind communities is extensive, beginning with Paul Jacobs, "Clouds from Nevada," *Reporter*, May 16, 1957, 10–29; the best include Ball, *Justice Downwind*; Philip L. Fradkin, *Fallout: An American Nuclear Tragedy* (Tucson: University of Arizona Press, 1989); Carole Gallagher, *American Ground Zero: The Secret Nuclear War* (New York: Random House, 1993). Stephen Hilgartner, Richard C. Bell, and Rory O'Connor, *Nukespeak: The Selling of Nuclear Technologies in America* (San Francisco: Sierra Club Books, 1982), is a brilliant study of nuclear propaganda presented to the American public; see 84–100.

5. Diane Nielson, quoted in Gallagher, *American Ground Zero*, 147.

6. U.S. Atomic Energy Commission (AEC), *Assuring Public Safety in Continental Weapons Tests* (Washington, D.C.: GPO, 1953), 78–83.

7. AEC, *Assuring Public Safety*, 81; AEC, *The Effects of High-Yield Nuclear Weapons* (Washington, D.C.: GPO, 1955), 16.

8. Leonard Slater, "The World Blew Up," *Newsweek*, February 19, 1951, 25.

9. Fradkin, *Fallout*, 126.

10. AEC, *Atomic Tests in Nevada* (Washington, D.C.: GPO, 1955).

11. AEC, *Atomic Tests*, 37–38. See also the film *Atomic Tests in Nevada* (Lookout Mt. Films, 1954).

12. AEC, *Atomic Tests*, 15.

13. AEC, *Atomic Tests*, 2.

14. AEC, *Atomic Tests*, 35, 39.

15. John L. Balderston Jr. and Gordon W. Hewes, *Atomic Attack—A Manual for Survival* (Culver City, Calif.: Murray & Gee, 1950), 25. Published under the auspices of the Council on Atomic Implications of the University of Southern California, this booklet was written by a USC anthropologist (Hewes) and a physicist (Balderston). From 1947 to 1948, Balderston was an assistant director of the Association of Scientists for Atomic Education.

16. Needless to say, this practice only helped to legitimize the routine overexposure of test-site workers. AEC, *Assuring Public Safety*, 113.

17. AEC, *Atomic Tests*, 11, 13–14, 2.

18. "You Go to Desert Rock," *Armed Forces Talk*, September 19, 1952, 13. Desert Rock was the name given to exercises that included the presence of military personnel in atomic tests in Nevada. These exercises were all staged from Camp Mercury, a permanent installation adjacent to the NTS.

19. MSgt. Roy E. Heinecke, with graphics by Sgt. Vance Bristow, "You Versus the A-Bomb," *Leatherneck*, August 1953, 32.

20. Gallagher, *American Ground Zero*, 75.

21. "The Survivor," *Army Combat Forces Journal*, February 1955, 35.

22. General John E. Dahlquist, "We Will Survive If We Have Leadership," *Army*, February 1956, 35.

23. Heinecke, "You Versus the A-Bomb," 33.

24. "You Go to Desert Rock," 2, 13, 15.

25. "When an A-Bomb Falls," *Army Information Digest*, April 1950, 23.

26. AEC, *Atomic Test*, 11.

27. "Statement by Lewis L. Strauss, Chairman United States Atomic Energy Commission," in AEC, *Effects of High-Yield Nuclear Explosions*, 7.

28. "Atomic Light in the Desert . . . and Answers to Fearful Questions People Ask," *Newsweek*, March 21, 1955, 31.

29. AEC, *Atomic Tests*, 23.

30. *Washington Post*, November 17, 1949, 1; for another example see *New York Times*, April 1, 1954, 20.

31. Major General Emerson C. Itschner, "Blueprint for a Quick Recovery," *Army*, July 1958, 55.

32. Colonel William B. Bunker, "Another Job for the Army," *Army Combat Forces Journal* 5:8 (March 1955): 34.

33. Colonel George C. Reinhardt, "Don't Wait for the H-bomb," *Marine Corps Gazette*, January 1952, 35.

34. Lieutenant Colonel Arthur W. Milberg, "Atomic War Questions for Battle Commanders," *Army*, January 1959, 26. A 1957 article in *Army* advocated "Winning with Your Wounded." The authors suggested that in the face of immense casualties after a nuclear attack, military doctors may have to make a "dramatic reappraisal of current concepts regarding 'effective' versus 'non-effective' soldiers" in deciding which of the wounded to evacuate and which to return to active duty; see Lieutenant Colonels Spurgeon H. Neel Jr. and James B. Hartgering, "Win With Your Wounded," *Army*, October 1957, 22.

35. "The President's News Conference of June 25, 1957," *Public Papers of the Presidents: Dwight D. Eisenhower, 1957* (Washington, D.C.: GPO, 1958), 498–99.

36. "Atomic Light in the Desert," 25–27. The AEC admits on page 27 of the Green Book that "increasing the height of the towers helps to reduce fallout, and in the 1955 series they were extended from 300 to 500 feet. Such height required very strong steel towers, and the large quantity of metal used became part of the radioactive debris, offsetting under some circumstances much of the advantage of the greater height."

37. Hewlett and Holl, *Atoms for Peace*, 398–402.

38. Eisenhower, "President's News Conference," 498–99; for other statements in the "clean bomb" campaign, see news conferences of July 3, 1957, April 9 and 30, 1958; statement by President Eisenhower of March 26, 1958; and the speech by Secretary John Foster Dulles to the United Nations General Assembly of September 19, 1957.

39. JCS 1691/3, June 30, 1947, 57–89.

40. JCS 1691/3.

41. JCS 1691/3.

42. JCS 1691/3.

43. JSAC 508, February 15, 1950, "A Study on Patterns of War in the Atomic Warfare Age."

44. Op-36C/jm, March 18, 1954, quoted in David Alan Rosenberg, "A Smoking, Radiating Ruin at the End of Two Hours," *International Security* 6:3 (Winter 1981/82): 18–28. There is evidence that President Eisenhower also considered a "defensive" first strike as a realistic option; see Item #61, Memorandum of Discussion at the 277th Meeting of the National Security Council, Washington, February 27, 1956, in *Foreign Relations*, XIX (1955–57), 204.

6. The Atomic Kid: American Children vs. the Bomb

1. Robert Cahn, "A Is for Atom," *Collier's*, June 21, 1952, 16.
2. Cahn, "A Is for Atom."
3. There is extensive scholarship examining the focus of the efforts made by the Federal Civil Defense Administration to reach both the American family and children in school settings, but almost none on efforts aimed at children as individuals. For discussions of civil defense efforts focused on family and school, see Margot Henriksen, *Dr. Strangelove's America: Society and Culture in the Atomic Age* (Berkeley: University of California Press, 1997), 108–11; Laura McEnaney, *Civil Defense Begins at Home: Militarization Meets Everyday Life in the Fifties* (Princeton: Princeton University Press, 2000), 68–87; Guy Oakes, *The Imaginary War: Civil Defense and American Cold War Culture* (New York: Oxford University Press, 1994), 105–17; Spencer Weart, *Nuclear Fear: A History of Images* (Cambridge, Mass.: Harvard University Press, 1988), 129–37; Kenneth D. Rose, *One Nation Underground: The Fallout Shelter in American Culture* (New York: New York University Press, 2001), 126–40; JoAnne Brown, "A Is for *Atom*, B Is for *Bomb*: Civil Defense in American Public Education," *Journal of American History* 75:1 (June 1988): 68–90.
4. See *The Public Papers of the Presidents: Dwight D. Eisenhower, 1960–1961* (Washington, D.C.: GPO, 1961), 1034–40.
5. Michael Scheibach, *Atomic Narratives and American Youth: Coming of Age with the Atom, 1945–1955* (Jefferson, N.C.: McFarland, 2003), 7.
6. Tom Engelhardt, *The End of Victory Culture: Cold War America and the Disillusioning of a Generation* (New York: Basic Books, 1995), 7.
7. Engelhardt, *End of Victory Culture*, 7–8.
8. Engelhardt, *End of Victory Culture*, 9.
9. *Duck and Cover*, dir. Anthony Rizzo, prod. Leo M. Langlois (Archer Films, 1951). See also "Civil Defense Film for Schools," *Elementary School Journal*, September 1951, 12.
10. Henriksen, *Dr. Strangelove's America*, 107.
11. *The Atomic Café*, dir. and prod. Jayne Loader, Kevin Rafferty, Pierce Rafferty (The Archives Project, 1982).
12. August 29, 1949, in Semipalatinsk, Kazakhstan. This test is commonly referred to in the West as Joe 1.
13. The jingle writers were Leo Carr and Leon Corday, with Leo Langlois. See "Putting the Jingle in Bert: Post Production," *Duck and Cover: The Citizen Kane of Civil Defense*, www.conelrad.com/duckandcover/cover.php?turtle=01 (accessed April 2, 2009).
14. This and the following quotes are taken from the soundtrack of *Duck and Cover*.

15. The single exception to this absence of adults is a scene of a family at a picnic; when the flash occurs, the children scramble under the picnic blanket while the father fall to the ground and covers his head with a newspaper.

16. William M. Lamers, "Identification for School Children," *NEA Journal* 41:2 (February 1952): 99. In "A Is for *Atom*," JoAnne Brown shows that the integration of civil defense segments into public-school curricula served professional as well as civic purposes.

17. Albert Furtwangler, "Growing Up Nuclear," *Bulletin of the Atomic Scientists* 37:1 (January 1981): 44.

18. *Atomic Alert (Elementary Version)* (Encyclopedia Britannica Films Inc., 1951). The film was made in collaboration with the Institute for Nuclear Studies at the University of Chicago.

19. For discussions of nuclear devastation in science fiction books, see David Dowling, *Fictions of Nuclear Disaster* (Iowa City: University of Iowa Press, 1987), 43–113; Albert E. Stone, *Literary Aftershocks: American Writers, Readers, and the Bomb* (New York: Twayne, 1994), 33–65; Paul Brians, *Nuclear Holocausts: Atomic War in Fiction, 1895–1984* (Kent, Ohio: Kent State University Press, 1987).

20. Dean Owen, *End of the World* (New York: Ace Publishing, 1952). Owen's book was turned into the 1962 film *Panic in Year Zero*, discussed in chapter 4.

21. *Atomic City*, dir. Jerry Hooper, prod. Joseph Sistrom (Paramount Pictures, 1952).

22. Robert K. Musil, "Growing Up Nuclear," *Bulletin of the Atomic Scientists* 38:1 (January 1982): 19. At the time, Musil was both an antinuclear activist and a lecturer in American Studies at Temple University. He was writing in response to the earlier article by Furtwanger.

23. Richard Rhodes, introduction to *Face to Face with the Bomb* by Paul Shambroom (Baltimore: John Hopkins University Press, 2003), xi. See also Rhodes's *The Making of the Atomic Bomb* (New York: Simon and Schuster, 1986).

24. Michael J. Carey, "Psychological Fallout," *Bulletin of the Atomic Scientists* 38:1 (January 1982): 20. See also Michael J. Carey, "The Schools and Civil Defense: The Fifties Revisited," *Teachers College Record* 84:1 (Fall 1982): 115–27. Carey's work is summarized in Robert Jay Lifton and Richard Falk, *Indefensible Weapons: The Political and Psychological Case against Nuclearism* (New York: Basic Books, 1982), 48–56.

25. Carey, "Psychological Fallout," 21.

26. Carey, "Psychological Fallout," 22.

27. Todd Gitlin, *The Sixties: Years of Hope, Days of Rage* (New York: Bantam, 1987), 22.

28. Milton Schwebel, "Nuclear Cold War: Student Opinions and Professional Responsibility," in *Behavioral Science and Human Survival*, ed. Milton Schwebel (Palo Alto, Calif.: Science and Behavior Books, 1965), 210.

29. Schwebel, "Nuclear Cold War," 212.

30. Sibylle K. Escalona, "Children and the Threat of Nuclear War," in Child Study Association of America, *Children and the Threat of Nuclear War* (New York: Duell, Sloan and Pearce, 1964), 3–24.

31. Musil, "Growing Up Nuclear," 19.

32. See Mick Broderick, "Rebels *with* a Cause: Children versus the Military Industrial Complex," in *Youth Culture in Global Cinema*, ed. Timothy Shary and Alexandria Seibel (Austin: University of Texas Press, 2007), 37–55.

33. Peter Biskind, *Seeing Is Believing* (New York: Pantheon, 1983), 23–36.

34. *The Blob*, dir. Irwin S. Yeaworth Jr., prod. Jack H. Harris (Paramount Pictures, 1958). The following quotes and incidents are taken from the film.

35. The salvation of the world is cast in doubt, however. The words "The End" in the final frame of the film morph into a question mark.

36. Todd Gitlin, himself a former activist, remarks that "to many in my generation, especially the incipient New Left, the grimmest and least acknowledged underside of affluence was the Bomb. . . . We grew up taking cover in school drills—the first American generation compelled from infancy to fear not only war but the end of days." *The Sixties*, 22.

37. Students for a Democratic Society (SDS), *The Port Huron Statement* (Chicago: Charles H. Kerr, 1990).

38. SDS, *Port Huron*. See also Scheibach, *Atomic Narratives*, 15–16.

Index

ROBERT JACOBS is an assistant professor at the Hiroshima Peace Institute at Hiroshima City University. Born in Miami, Florida, Jacobs received his PhD in the history of science and technology from the University of Illinois at Urbana–Champaign in 2004. He is the editor of the book *Filling the Hole in the Nuclear Future: Art and Popular Culture Respond to the Bomb* (2010) and has published on nuclear history and culture in the *Journal of American Culture, Interdisciplinary Humanities, and Intersections: Gender and Sexuality in Asia and the Pacific,* among other places. He is the father of four grown children and lives with his wife, Carol, in Hiroshima, Japan.